INTERActions

SMALL GROUP SERIES

Evangelism

BECOMING STRONGER SALT AND BRIGHTER LIGHT

D1456497

INTERActions

SMALL GROUP SERIES

Evangelism

BECOMING STRONGER SALT AND BRIGHTER LIGHT

BILL HYBELS

WITH KEVIN & SHERRY HARNEY

WILLOW
CREEK
RESOURCES

ZondervanPublishingHouse

Grand Rapids, Michigan

A Division of HarperCollins*Publishers*

Evangelism
Copyright © 1996 by the Willow Creek Association

Requests for information should be addressed to:

🏢 ZondervanPublishingHouse
Grand Rapids, Michigan 49530

ISBN: 0-310-20678-2

Zondervan Editors: Jack Kuhatschek and Rachel Boers
Willow Creek Editors: Bill Donahue and Mark Mittelberg
Interior design by Rick Devon

Printed in the United States of America

98 99 00 01 02 03 /❖ DC/ 10 9 8 7 6 5

CONTENTS

INTERACTIONS

In 1992, Willow Creek Community Church, in partnership with Zondervan Publishing House and the Willow Creek Association, released a curriculum for small groups entitled the Walking with God Series. In just three years, almost a half million copies of these small group study guides were being used in churches around the world. The phenomenal response to this curriculum affirmed the need for relevant and biblical small group materials.

At the writing of this curriculum, there are over 1,000 small groups meeting regularly within the structure of Willow Creek Community Church. We believe this number will increase as we continue to place a central value on small groups. Many other churches throughout the world are growing in their commitment to small group ministries as well, so the need for resources is increasing.

In response to this great need, the Interactions small group series has been developed. Willow Creek Association and Zondervan Publishing House have joined together to create a whole new approach to small group materials. These discussion guides are meant to challenge group members to a deeper level of sharing, to create lines of accountability, to move followers of Christ into action, and to help group members become fully devoted followers of Christ.

SUGGESTIONS FOR INDIVIDUAL STUDY

1. Begin each session with prayer. Ask God to help you understand the passage and apply it to your life.
2. A good modern translation, such as the New International Version, the New American Standard Bible, or the New Revised Standard Version, will give you the most help. Questions in this guide are based on the New International Version.
3. Read and reread the passage(s). You must know what the passage says before you can understand what it means and how it applies to you.
4. Write your answers in the spaces provided in the study guide. This will help you to express clearly your understanding of the passage.

5. Keep a Bible dictionary handy. Use it to look up unfamiliar words, names, or places.

SUGGESTIONS FOR GROUP STUDY

1. Come to the session prepared. Careful preparation will greatly enrich your time in group discussion.
2. Be willing to join in the discussion. The leader of the group will not be lecturing, but will encourage people to discuss what they have learned in the passage. Plan to share what God has taught you in your individual study.
3. Stick to the passage being studied. Base your answers on the verses being discussed rather than on outside authorities such as commentaries or your favorite author or speaker.
4. Try to be sensitive to the other members of the group. Listen attentively when they speak, and be affirming whenever you can. This will encourage more hesitant members of the group to participate.
5. Be careful not to dominate the discussion. By all means participate! But allow others to have equal time.
6. If you are the discussion leader, you will find additional suggestions and helpful ideas in the leader's notes.

ADDITIONAL RESOURCES AND TEACHING MATERIALS

At the end of this study guide you will find a collection of resources and teaching materials to help you in your growth as a follower of Christ. You will also find resources that will help your church develop and build fully devoted followers of Christ.

Introduction:
Becoming Stronger
Salt and Brighter Light

Without pretending to be a professional mind reader, I can make an educated guess as to what you might be thinking as you prepare to begin this series entitled *Evangelism: Becoming Stronger Salt and Brighter Light.* Some of you are delighted. You have been waiting to dig into this topic for years. You are eager to improve your personal evangelistic skills. You are anxious to learn some new methods and strategies. In fact, you are already thinking of some people you might be able to share Christ with once you get a little more training under your belt.

Others of you are rather neutral on the subject of evangelism because you don't know what to expect from this study series. You might even be waiting to see how the first session goes to decide if you are going to stick with this study all the way through six sessions. You are open to the truth of God's Word and you are seeking the leading of the Spirit of God. Although you may have a little apprehension, you have decided to approach this study with a teachable spirit and a willing heart.

Some of you may be starting this study with a sense of dread. Just hearing the phrase "personal evangelism" strikes terror in your heart. Perhaps in your past you were subjected to a form of teaching that overemphasized personal evangelism to the point where spirituality was determined by how often and how effectively you shared your faith. If this was the case, you may be dealing with feelings of fear, pressure, and maybe even guilt.

Like many others, I have had experiences where the pressure to enter into personal evangelism was put on me in an unhealthy way. Some years ago, I attended a conference in a small town. Late on the final evening of the conference, the speaker told those of us in attendance that if we really loved Jesus Christ and if we really cared for people who were facing an eternity in hell, every one of us would make a commitment to share Jesus Christ with at least three people before we went to bed.

I looked at my watch. It was already about 10 P.M., and it was a very small town. I started thinking of my 7 A.M. flight back to Chicago the next day and decided I just couldn't meet the challenge. To heighten the pressure, the speaker asked everyone who would take this evangelistic challenge to stand to their feet as a sign of their commitment. I think I was the only one who didn't stand up to publically accept the challenge. As I sat there with all the rest of the people standing, I felt singled out, pressured, guilty, and ostracized.

Some of you have experienced those kinds of abuses, and some of those old feelings are already beginning to surface as you think about beginning this study. Those of you with more introverted temperaments may especially be fearing the worst. You may be wondering, *Is this study filled with the same old pressure tactics I've faced before? Am I going to end up feeling like a failure? Is this going to be six studies that heap guilt on me for not being the world's greatest evangelist?*

Friends, I want to assure you at the very beginning, I have no desire to increase your burden or pressure level when it comes to communicating your faith. You can grow and learn how to be an effective evangelist no matter what your background, personality, or temperament. It doesn't matter if you are extroverted or introverted. God has wonderful plans to use you as an evangelist just the way you are.

In the following sessions, we will first look at two central metaphors for evangelism: salt and light. These images will help us begin to see our place as God's evangelists in the world. Next, we will look at the issue of the motivation behind personal evangelism. What gets us moving into the world with the Good News of Jesus? In the third session we will get inside the mind-set of an evangelist. We will see how our whole life focus should be transformed by the call to be "fishers of men." The fourth topic will be the message of the evangelist. Here we will look at some simple and clear ways we can help others know what Jesus has done for them. In the fifth and sixth sessions we will discover the various styles of an evangelist. Each of us is made differently, and we need to learn to use the method and style that works for us. Every single evangelist has his or her own style. You will find freedom and liberty in sharing your faith when you come to grips with the particular style God intended for you.

My prayer is for you to grow in your understanding of what it means to be light in a world of darkness and salt in a world that has lost its flavor. No matter what your starting point, I believe this study can result in your having a whole new commitment to tell others about the Good News of Jesus.

You are the salt of the earth.
But if the salt loses its saltiness,
how can it be made salty again?
It is no longer good for anything,
except to be thrown out and trampled by men.
You are the light of the world.
A city on a hill cannot be hidden.
Neither do people light a lamp and put it under a bowl.
Instead they put it on its stand,
and it gives light to everyone in the house.
In the same way, let your light shine before men,
that they may see your good deeds
and praise your Father in heaven.

MATTHEW 5:13–16

Bill Hybels

Some of the material in the study guide has been adapted from the book *Becoming a Contagious Christian,* by Bill Hybels and Mark Mittelberg. To further deepen your understanding of relational evangelism you may want to read this book. (See the information pages in the back of this book.)

BEING SALT AND LIGHT

The metaphors of salt and light are two of the most frequently used pictures in Scripture that describe what Christians ought to be. In Matthew 5:13–16, we find the most well-known passage on this topic. Here Jesus clearly calls His followers to let their lights shine and to let their lives be salty. The verses preceding Jesus' words about light and salt are called the Beatitudes. In Matthew 5:1–12, Jesus looks at His followers and says, "I want to describe to you how you ought to behave and what your attitudes ought to be in the family." And then He speaks these famous words: "Blessed are the poor in spirit, for theirs is the kingdom of heaven." In other words, Jesus wants His family members to walk in humility—in deep awareness of their need for grace.

Think about the words Jesus then speaks to His followers. He says, "I hope you act poor in spirit toward each other. I hope you have the ability to mourn over sin and sadness. I hope you can meet each other at the points of pain and brokenness in the family. I hope there's a gentleness and a kindness that sweeps through your community of faith. And I hope there is a hunger and a thirst for righteousness among My people. I hope there is a pureness of heart. I hope there are peacemakers in the family who take reconciliation seriously. I hope there is courage to withstand trials and persecution for My sake." He continues, "My people should relate to Me and to each other in distinctively Spirit-anointed ways. There are certain things that should mark the relationships of those who are part of My family."

Right after all these words of encouragement for believers, Jesus adds, "Now, I am also terribly concerned about people *outside* the family. Lost people matter to Me, and I am deeply concerned about how you relate to them." Think about that.

Jesus is saying that the most persuasive and compelling argument for salvation He can present to an *outsider* is a close-up view of the transformed life of one of His *insiders*. Nothing packs a punch like a genuinely transformed life. At this point, Jesus gives us the two famous metaphors: "My children, each and every one of you should see yourselves as salt and light to people outside the family."

A WIDE ANGLE VIEW

1 What qualities or characteristics of salt are valuable and helpful?

What qualities or characteristics of light are valuable and helpful?

A BIBLICAL PORTRAIT

Read Matthew 5:13–16

2 What parallels do you see between both light and salt and your role as an evangelist in the world?

How are you to be like light?

How are you to be like salt?

SHARPENING THE FOCUS

Read Snapshot "An Equation for Evangelism:
(HP + CP + CC = MI)"

AN EQUATION FOR EVANGELISM: (HP + CP + CC = MI)

Let's break with mathematic tradition and start by talking about the *answer* to this equation. What does MI mean? It means *maximum impact*. There is no mystery about the fact that Christ longed for His followers to have maximum impact on people outside the family. The end result of effective evangelism is maximum influence on those who are seeking spiritual truth.

Now let's look at the front end of the formula. What might HP plus CP plus CC mean in relation to our being salt and light? HP stands for *high potency*, CP stands for *close proximity*, and CC stands for *clear communication*. What begins to emerge from this text in Matthew is Jesus' concern about the impact our lives should make on others. In order for maximum impact (MI) to happen, something with a lot of power (HP) must get real close (CP) to something that needs to be influenced. However, in addition to being within proximity (CP), we must also communicate (CC) the message of God's love. See the formula shaping up? Jesus said someone with high potency (HP) has to be willing to get into close proximity (CP) to someone else and clearly communicate (CC) the message of Jesus if maximum influence (MI) is going to happen. Jesus chose the metaphors of salt and light because they both follow this same formula.

3 What can you do to increase your potency as a Christian?

4 What can you do to increase your proximity to seekers in the course of a regular week?

5 How would you evaluate your life in light of this equation?

How would you evaluate the lives of your church members in light of this equation?

6

If followers of Christ are going to have a potency level high enough to impact seekers, there are some specific qualities that will need to be in their lives. Why is each of the characteristics listed below essential in the lives of fully devoted followers of Christ if they are to have maximum impact with the Gospel?

- Spiritual confidence

- An authentic faith

- An urgency about the Gospel

Read Snapshot "Spiritual Disciplines"

SPIRITUAL DISCIPLINES

Where do spiritually salty Christians get their confidence, sincerity, and sense of urgency? Where do they learn to shine so brightly? I wish I could give you a spine-tingling, bungy-jumping kind of answer, but it's actually pretty simple. They get it from the age-old, daily, personal, spiritual disciplines that have made believers salty for a couple of thousand years.

When the spotlights aren't on them . . . when they're not at church . . . when no one is looking, these salty Christians are thinking about Christ. They each have a holy place where they meet with Christ, where they open their Bibles and just let the Word of God speak to them. They pray more than other people pray, because they know the power of prayer. They have close relationships with brothers and sisters in Christ who help them negotiate life and faith. They use their spiritual gifts, and they're out sharing their faith when no one is looking. They're not grandstanding; they're just conveying Christ. In the middle of all this, God meets them and adds a little bit to the savoriness of their lives. And as they live in the presence of God, they begin to shine a little more brightly.

7 Why is strength in the spiritual disciplines mandatory for high potency?

8 How are you doing in practicing daily spiritual disciplines at this time in your life?

9 What specific spiritual discipline(s) do you need to develop in your life at this time?

What is one way your group members can help you grow in this spiritual discipline?

PUTTING YOURSELF IN THE PICTURE

MAKING AN IMPACT LIST

Take time this week to make a list of three people with whom you are in close proximity. It is important to build relationships and friendships with people without strings attached, to be willing to love them no matter how they respond to Jesus. The fact that they matter to God and matter to you should be enough.

Impact List:

- _____
- _____
- _____

Take time this week to pray for:

Seekers—Ask God to draw them to Himself, to open their eyes to the condition of their lives, and to help them see their need for forgiveness and grasp the meaning of the Cross.

Yourself—Ask God to help you live an attractive and authentic Christian life. Ask Him to also help you have the wisdom and knowledge necessary to share the Gospel.

THE MOTIVATION FOR EVANGELISM

REFLECTIONS FROM SESSION 1

1. Who is one of the people on your Impact List you are praying for? What has happened in your heart as you have prayed for this person on a regular basis?
2. Has God opened a door for you to share your faith with someone on your Impact List over the past week? If so, how did you respond? If the opening has not yet been presented, what opportunities do you see in the near future? How can you build relational bridges with people to increase your proximity factor?

THE BIG PICTURE

Why share our faith with others? Why devote time to studying personal evangelism? Why has evangelism been a central focus of Christians throughout time?

First, we communicate the life-changing message of Christ because our Savior is an amazing God who has given us love and hope and the promise of eternity. A stockpile of God's blessings have been poured into our lives. When we live in the awareness of all God has given us, it spills over to others.

Second, we share our faith because we have been honored with a heavenly invitation to participate in this grand endeavor to bring people to faith. The God of heaven has invited all followers of Christ to share in the most important enterprise ever—to help irreligious people become fully devoted followers of Christ. It is an honor to be His agent.

Third, we share our faith because hell is real. There are people who are headed for a Christless eternity if they don't come to know Jesus. The eternal destinies of seekers should matter to us. After all, they matter to God!

Fourth, we share our faith because whenever we do have the occasion to lead someone to Christ, we experience a fresh awareness of the fact that Jesus and the angels in heaven are rejoicing. What a joy-filled moment when somebody says, "Thanks for leading me to Jesus—thanks for all of eternity!" Leading someone to the Cross is the single greatest contribution you can ever make to someone's life. When God uses you to bring someone to Christ, your life will never be the same.

A WIDE ANGLE VIEW

1 How have those around you communicated their faith to you? What motivated them to take the risk of communicating their faith?

2 When have you had the privilege to clearly explain the Gospel message to someone? How did you do it? What was your motive for doing so?

Read Acts 1:6–8

3 This passage makes it clear that God's plan is to use His followers to spread the message of salvation. How do you feel when you realize God's plan to reach the world relies on your willingness to be His messenger?

SHARPENING THE FOCUS

Read Snapshot "The Stockpile Factor"

THE STOCKPILE FACTOR

When mature believers have a proper understanding of their spiritual inheritance, they cannot stop this knowledge from spilling over into other people's lives. One of the most effective ways to be an evangelist is to manage your life in such a way as to stay mindful of your inheritance in Christ. Stay ever aware of the character of God. Never forget the magnitude of the transformation that has taken strangers and converted them into sons and daughters of God. Live with a profound thankfulness for the size of your spiritual stockpile, the sheer scope of your blessings in Christ. When this happens, it will take very little effort or motivation to reach out to lost people and say, "You need to come and see how wonderful God is."

This kind of evangelism is exceedingly effective. When a true believer looks an unbeliever in the eye and says, "Taste and see that the God of history is good," or when a follower of Christ says to a seeker, "I don't know about you, but as for me and my house, because of how wonderful God is, we are going to serve the Lord," those words have a way of striking a responsive chord in the lives of unbelievers.

---

4 What are some of the blessings you have received and riches you have inherited since you became a child of God?

Does your awareness of this stockpile of blessings motivate you to share your faith? If so, how? If not, why do you think it has no motivational power on you?

Read Snapshot "A Heavenly Honor"

A HEAVENLY HONOR

 Another motivation for personal evangelism is the honor of being an agent of God. Before returning to heaven, Jesus told His followers that they would be His messengers, His ambassadors, His witnesses. Jesus wanted His followers to realize that His plan to reach the world depended on them. What an honor! What a responsibility! You are Plan A in God's strategy to reach the world. And there is no Plan B. God uses individuals as His spokespeople. He has placed the message of salvation in your hands and you have the high honor of bringing the Good News to the ends of the earth.

5 How does it feel to be honored by God with the responsibility of proclaiming the Gospel message?

Does this responsibility motivate or overwhelm you? Why?

6 How does the Holy Spirit work to ignite the evangelistic flame in each of us? How does He help us share the truth of Christ?

Read Snapshot "The Reality of Hell"

THE REALITY OF HELL

 A third motivation for becoming an effective evangelist is not one people like to talk about, but we need to deal with it honestly. Another very sobering motivation for becoming an effective evangelist is the reality of hell. Now, you may hate thinking about that. But the plain truth is, hell is a reality, and real people go there for eternity. There are people who will face a Christless eternity if they don't find forgiveness in Christ. The reality of hell was a major theme in the evangelistic ministry of Jesus. We read time after time of Jesus' sorrow over a lack of response to this life-giving message. He knew the stakes were skyhigh with eternity hanging in the balance, and we must live with that same sobering realization.

7

What feelings do you experience when you read in the Bible about the reality of hell and eternal separation from God?

When you read through the names of people on your Impact List, how does the reality of hell act as a motivation for evangelism?

Read Snapshot "The Joy of Salvation"

THE JOY OF SALVATION

A final motivation for evangelism is the reward of leading someone to Christ. To experience the thrill of having a person look you in the eye and say to you, "You know, I was on the road headed for hell, and God used you to bring me to Himself." To hear someone say, "I needed an ambassador. I needed a credible witness. I needed someone whose life matched his message, and you were that person for me. Thanks for being an evangelist. Thanks for reaching out to me. Thanks for answering my questions. Thanks for putting up with my rebellion. Thanks for loving me at a time when I wasn't particularly loveable. Jesus saved me, but you led me to the Cross where I found grace."

Once you hear those words and gaze into those tear-filled eyes, you will never be the same. The passion to reach out grows when you experience the joy of seeing a seeker become a devoted follower of Christ. Nothing compares!

8

Describe the joy you experience when a seeker comes to faith in Jesus Christ.

What happens in heaven?

How can this joy be a motivation to communicate your faith with others?

9 Who would you like to reach out to with the love of Jesus?

What is one thing you can do to extend the love of Jesus to this person in the coming week?

PUTTING YOURSELF IN THE PICTURE

TAKING A LOOK AT YOUR STOCKPILE

Take time in the coming week to make a list of the spiritual blessings you have received because of your faith in Jesus Christ. Think about all God has done for you, His provision in your life, the changes He has made, the hope of eternity, the fruit of the Spirit (Gal. 5:22–23), the meaningful relationships He has given you, and any other things that are in your stockpile of God's goodness.

- _____
- _____
- _____
- _____
- _____
- _____
- _____

- _____

- _____

- _____

- _____

- _____

- _____

- _____

(You may need to get a fresh piece of paper if this list fills up. Take time each day to keep adding to this list.)

Who are a few of the people you would love to see receive this same kind of stockpile of God's blessings and goodness?

- _____

- _____

- _____

- _____

Take time in the coming week to praise God for all of the good things He has given to you and done for you. Also, pray for those seekers who have yet to know Jesus. They need His love, forgiveness, and stockpile as much as you do!

THE EVANGELIST'S MIND-SET

REFLECTIONS FROM SESSION 2

1. What are some of the things in your spiritual stockpile you are thanking God for at this time in your life? How does thinking about these things impact the way you look at seekers?

2. Did you have a chance to tell a seeker about some of the things in your spiritual stockpile over the past few days? If so, how did they respond? If not, who could you tell in the coming week?

THE BIG PICTURE

Along a beautiful inland sea walked a teacher by the name of Jesus. As He walked along the shore of the Sea of Galilee, He spotted two men with fishing nets casting their nets into the sea, hoping to catch fish to bring to the local fish market. These two men, Peter and Andrew, had done this almost every day of their lives. It was their livelihood, their occupation, the key to their daily survival. In fact, it's probably safe to say that fishing was the single most important pursuit in Peter and Andrew's lives.

Over the years, the two men had become good at fishing. There is little question that their whole mind-set toward life had been shaped by their commitment to their livelihood. When they got up in the morning, they most likely discussed with one another where they would fish that day, what nets they would use, how long they planned to stay out, and how much money they might make at the market when they sold their fish.

Jesus approached these two men and said to them, "Follow Me, and I will make you fishers of men." Now, this command was not just about fishing. At the heart of it all, Jesus was challenging Peter and Andrew to consider a total life and worldview transformation. A complete change in their mind-set. In a way, Jesus was saying, "Peter, Andrew, up to this moment your whole life has revolved around fishing, where to catch fish, how to catch fish, and how to market fish. A day doesn't pass when the two of you don't put your heads together and discuss various ways in which you can become more effective at catching fish. But hear Me well, if you follow Me, trust Me, and find new life in Me, you will learn how much men and women matter to Me, and you will allow Me to make you fishers of men."

Jesus wanted these two hardworking, committed fishermen to realize there was an infinitely more significant endeavor in life than catching fish. It is fine to make a living. We all need to take our professions very seriously. We need to do our work for the glory of God. But be reminded that there is something far more important than catching fish and bringing them to the market. More important than any career or vocation is the call to capture the attention of sinful men and women and to bring them to the cross of Christ. There is no higher calling in life. There is no greater challenge. There is no more significant task in all the world.

A WIDE ANGLE VIEW

1 If you could design a dream job and be successful at it, what would it be?

Why would you choose this vocation?

2 What is the major vocational pursuit in your life? (This can range from being a homemaker to pursuing an education.)

What makes this pursuit valuable to you?

A BIBLICAL PORTRAIT

Read Matthew 4:18–20

3 Describe the differences between being fishermen and being fishers of men.

What are some of the similarities?

4 How did Jesus' invitation change the lives of Peter and Andrew?

How has the invitation to follow Jesus changed your life?

Read Snapshot "The People Business"

THE PEOPLE BUSINESS

Jesus wanted Peter and Andrew to know that the most important business on the face of this planet is the people business. Jesus was a carpenter; He knew the importance of all kinds of jobs. The fact is, the fish business, the construction business, the food business, the travel business, the insurance business, are all fine and necessary—but no earthly enterprise is as important as the business of bringing lost people to the cross of Christ. Jesus is telling all those who will follow Him that every other earthly activity pales by comparison with the significance of helping an individual man, woman, boy, or girl come into a liberating relationship with the God of the universe through Jesus Christ. In other words, the people business is the most important business in the world.

5

Have you come to the place in your life where you have realized that the people business is the most important business of all? If so, describe how you came to this realization. If not, what needs to be set aside so that the people business can be primary in your life?

Read Snapshot "What Sets Us Apart?"

WHAT SETS US APART?

Some time ago, I spent two days at a conference and ran into a man who had been thrust into the spotlight as the owner of a whole series of car dealerships on the East Coast. He is a committed follower of Christ. He sensed my interest in evangelism and pulled me aside and said, "I have to ask you a question that's driving me crazy." He said, "I have never told this to anybody else. I am a Christian, I love Jesus Christ with all my heart, soul, mind, and strength. I really do." Then he said, "I have been in the marketplace doing my job, being responsible, and leading a company with over 400 employees. As I review the last five years of my life in the marketplace, I can find no substantive difference in the way I function as compared to the way a moral humanitarian would function in the same job." He then said to me, "It seems there ought to be some kind of difference between us." I pressed him, saying, "What exactly do you mean?" He said, "A moral humanitarian, who may be an atheist, wants to be fair with his customers. So do I. A moral humanitarian wants to be sensitive to his employees. So do I. A moral humanitarian wants to have a good reputation in the community. So do I. A moral humanitarian wants to make a fair profit and not gouge people. So do I. I just don't see any big difference." Then he said, "There is no substantive difference between the way a moral humanitarian operates his business and the way I operate mine. Somehow, I think I ought to be making a bigger difference. I'm a Christian."

6 What would you have said to the Christian business owner in the story above?

What sets a Christian apart from a good moral person? What marks our lives and makes us distinct?

What makes a follower of Christ stand out in the market-place?

7 How do the following passages affirm that people are the most important pursuit in all of life?

Luke 4:14–21

Luke 14:12–14

Luke 15

Luke 19:1–10

8

What changes can you make in your life to shift some of your energy and focus away from the daily chores of fishing and onto the eternal work of fishing for people? How can you begin to shift priorities this week? How can we hold each other accountable to these commitments?

PUTTING YOURSELF IN THE PICTURE

An Honest Look at Fishing

Take time in the coming week to evaluate your commitment to fishing. First, think about your life vocation and pursuit. What are the things you have committed yourself to accomplishing or achieving? How are you working and developing skills to be successful in your life vocation?

Next, think about the pursuit of fishing for people. What are you doing to develop your skills to become successful in reaching lost people for Jesus? Finally, identify one or two ways you can sharpen and develop your skills as a fisher of men and women.

A Commitment to Memorize Scripture

"Come, follow me," Jesus said, "and I will make you fishers of men" (Matt. 4:19).

THE EVANGELIST'S MESSAGE

REFLECTIONS FROM SESSION 3

1. What have you done to develop your skills as a fisher of men and women since your last small group meeting?
2. If you memorized Matthew 4:19, how have these words of Jesus impacted you?

THE BIG PICTURE

A courtroom drama begins to unfold. You've seen dozens of these on TV. Closing arguments are presented by the two attorneys, and the jury goes into its deliberation. After what seems like days, they arrive at their critical, life-and-death decision. Everyone reassembles in the courtroom. The bailiff says "All rise." The judge enters. The judge directs the accused and says, "Will the defendant please rise?" The defendant comes to his feet, fearful and unsure. The judge asks the head juror, "Have you reached a verdict?" The response is clear, "We have, your honor." The words "Please read the verdict" are heard.

Tension is rising in the courtroom. The defendant is perspiring as the words are read: "We the jury," (pause for effect) "find the defendant," (drum roll). . . . The whole drama has been building up to the next few words. The wait is excruciating! What will the verdict be?

Movie makers and television producers know how to milk these moments for everything they're worth. They make for good drama and high ratings. Sometimes the verdict is "guilty," sometimes "not guilty." Sometimes they break for a commercial before they tell you, and you just about blow your stack! There is nothing like the high drama created in those few short moments when the message of guilty or not guilty is communicated at last.

A WIDE ANGLE VIEW

1 When have you waited what seemed like an eternity for some critical news or essential piece of information?

How did you feel during this time of waiting?

A BIBLICAL PORTRAIT

Read Acts 2:14–41

2 What kind of drama do you see unfolding in this passage?

What are the critical questions and issues found in Acts 2:14–41?

3 What elements of the Gospel did Peter share with the crowd when they cried out, "What shall we do?"

How are these elements still central to the way we present the message of Jesus to seekers today?

SHARPENING THE FOCUS

There is not one "correct" way to tell others about Jesus. Although the message never changes, we need to learn new ways to communicate the Good News of salvation in Christ. The apostle Peter said, "But in your hearts set apart Christ as Lord. Always be prepared to give an answer to everyone who asks you to give the reason for the hope that you have" (1 Peter 3:15). Although there are many ways to communicate the Gospel, in this session we will focus on four simple methods.

Read Snapshot "A Personal Testimony"

A PERSONAL TESTIMONY

The best way to rattle a seeker's cage is through the use of personal testimony. This is simply telling your story, relaying a concise description of your own journey to faith in Christ. Most people are willing, and actually glad, to hear someone share what their faith means to them. In this testimony, describe how you became a follower of Christ. Talk about the difference Jesus has made in your life. Tell another person about how great God is and what having faith in Jesus has done to change your life.

4

Take a few minutes to briefly tell your personal testimony to your group.

What difference has becoming a Christian made in your life?

Read Snapshot "Do vs. Done"

DO VS. DONE

Sometimes I'll say to a seeker, "If you'd ever be interested in discovering the difference between religion and Christianity, I'd be happy to explain it to you." Almost everyone is willing to pick up on that discussion. I explain that religion is spelled D-O. It is all about what we *do* to please God. We go to church, we give offerings, we try to be good, we follow the rules. The problem is, we never know if we have done enough. The reality is, we never can do enough.

Christianity is spelled D-O-N-E. Christianity is all about what Jesus has *done* for me. He came from heaven to earth, lived a perfect life, died on the cross for my sins, rose again, and offers us forgiveness and eternity in heaven. The focal point is on what Jesus has done for us, not what we do for Him. This is the difference between religion and Christianity.

5

Why does a religion of "doing" things always fall short?

When you hear that Jesus has "done" it all, how does that impact you? Why is relying solely on what Jesus has done the only way to heaven?

Read Snapshot "The Bridge"

THE BRIDGE

The bridge illustration works well because it can be drawn simply and clearly. In this illustration, there's a hill on one side, a chasm in the middle, and another hill on the other side. Sin separates a person from God. The result of trying to get to God on our own will be death—both physical and spiritual. There's only one way to cross the chasm of sin and that's the bridge. The cross of Jesus spans the distance between us and God the Father. Jesus Christ is the only way to God. When we trust in His death on the cross, we are freed from the power of sin and the judgment of death.

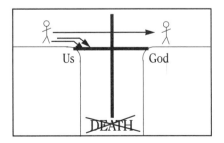

6 In what situation might you use this illustration to effectively communicate the message of salvation?

Read Snapshot "The Roman Road"

THE ROMAN ROAD

There is a classic three-step presentation of how to become a Christian often called The Roman Road, because it's all right in the Book of Romans.

This approach seems to be most effective when people are nearing a point of decision. At this point, they simply need a brief biblical explanation of the essence of Christianity. First, Romans 3:23 says, "For all have sinned and fall short of the glory of God." We must acknowledge our own sin. Second, Romans 6:23 says, "For the wages of sin is death, but the gift of God is eternal life in Christ Jesus our Lord." The wages, or payment, for our sins is death. However, the wonderful gift offered by God is forgiveness and eternal life in Jesus. Third, Romans 10:13 says, "Everyone who calls on the name of the Lord will be saved." When we call on Jesus for forgiveness, He will cleanse us, give us a new beginning, and help us live as His children forever.

7 What central elements of the Gospel are included in The Roman Road?

How can this simple, three-step presentation of the Gospel lead a person to new life in Jesus Christ?

8 Which of the four illustrations discussed in this session feels most comfortable and natural to you?

What is appealing to you about that particular illustration?

My Personal Testimony

Take time before your next meeting to write out your personal testimony. Who is Jesus Christ to you? What difference has He made in your life? What benefits and joys do you experience in your life because you are a follower of Christ? Use the space provided to write out your story of faith.

Practice Makes Perfect

Before your next meeting, link up with another group member and practice one of the other Gospel presentations. Which will you commit to learn and practice over the coming days: Do vs. Done, The Bridge, or The Roman Road? First, practice on your own. Then ask a group member or other Christian friend if you may practice on them. You will be surprised how quickly these approaches can be learned and incorporated into your daily life.

DISCOVERING YOUR STYLE: PART 1

REFLECTIONS FROM SESSION 4

1. For those of you who wrote out your testimony, would you be willing to read it to the group? What kind of person might this testimony speak to?
2. If you have been learning one of the other Gospel presentations, set up a time to practice it on the small group or the small group leader.

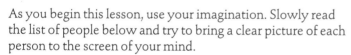

THE BIG PICTURE

As you begin this lesson, use your imagination. Slowly read the list of people below and try to bring a clear picture of each person to the screen of your mind.

What do you see when you think of:

- A librarian?
- A fighter pilot?
- A Sumo wrestler?
- A kindergarten teacher?
- A used car salesman?
- A ballet dancer?
- A doctor?
- An evangelist?

Each of these titles causes some kind of picture to form in our minds. Many of these images are positive, but some are not.

When some people think of a stereotypical evangelist, they picture an animated, extroverted, finger-pointing, Bible-pounding preacher who spews out hellfire and brimstone sermons. This is not an attractive picture. It certainly does not make the idea of being an evangelist very appealing to most followers of Christ.

Others may have an entirely different picture of an evangelist. They see a dynamic, powerful, eloquent communicator—a fluent and effective preacher of the Gospel like Billy Graham. Some picture an evangelist as a specially chosen person with rare and unique gifts that most "ordinary" Christians could never hope to duplicate.

What we *don't* see when we picture an evangelist is ourselves. Our mental image of an evangelist just doesn't match up with the person we see every morning in the mirror.

A WIDE ANGLE VIEW

1 What images come to your mind when you think about an evangelist?

Positive   *Negative*

Who are some effective evangelists you have known? What makes them effective?

A BIBLICAL PORTRAIT

Read Acts 17:16–34

2 How would you describe Paul's style of evangelism in this passage?

What made his approach effective?

SHARPENING THE FOCUS

Read Snapshot "Intellectual Style"

INTELLECTUAL STYLE

In Acts 17, the apostle Paul is trying to spread the message of Jesus Christ to philosophers and scholars of the city of Athens by *reasoning* in the synagogues with the Jews and the God-fearing Gentiles and in the marketplace with those who would listen. Some of the philosophers conversed and debated with him. As you read this passage, you will discover that Paul used an ingenious approach. He made reference to an altar in their city "to an unknown God" and then wove that into the thrust of his message.

Paul's approach was an intellectual one. A confrontational approach was not going to work with these philosophers. They needed to be presented with a thinking approach that appealed to their sense of reason, and Paul was the man for the job.

3 What are some values of an intellectual style of evangelism?

What are some possible problems with this approach?

4 How can a person with an intellectual style of evangelism develop their ability to effectively communicate their faith?

5 What kind of people can be reached with this style of evangelism?

Specifically, who are some people you know who might respond to this style of evangelism?

Read Snapshot "Confrontational Style"

CONFRONTATIONAL STYLE

The apostle Peter had a confrontational style of evangelism. In Acts 2:14, he took a stand, raised his voice and said, "Listen carefully to what I say." Then in verse 40 he tells the crowd that they crucified the wrong man—the Son of God. He then exhorted the crowd to repent, saying, "Save yourselves from this corrupt generation."

Peter's confrontational style was a frontal assault that required confidence and courage. And it was effective! Over 3,000 people trusted Christ after Peter shared the Gospel. The fact is, some people will only be reached when they are confronted courageously and straightforwardly with the message of Christ. Thankfully, some people are uniquely designed by God to be able to use a confrontational style of evangelism.

6 What are some advantages of a confrontational style of evangelism?

What are some possible problems with this approach?

7 How can a person with a confrontational style of evangelism develop their ability to more effectively communicate their faith?

8 What kind of people can be reached with this style of evangelism?

Specifically, who are some people who might respond to this style of evangelism?

Read Snapshot "Testimonial Style"

TESTIMONIAL STYLE

In the ninth chapter of the book of John there is a story of a blind man who was miraculously healed by Jesus. After his sight was restored, everyone kept asking about the one who healed him. They questioned him, saying, "Could it be the Messiah, the Son of God who healed you?" The man admitted he did not have all the answers to their questions, but told them what he knew for certain: "I was blind but now I see." It's as if he said, "Draw your own conclusions. I've drawn mine; I know who it was."

This is an example of a testimonial approach to evangelism. In this approach, someone experiences a miraculous transformation through the work of Jesus Christ and then simply looks for opportunities to tell their story to others. They're not very confrontational or oriented toward an intellectual approach, but they can tell their story. They can give their testimony. They can say, "I was spiritually blind, but now I see. Christ changed my life, and He can change yours."

---

9 What are some advantages of a testimonial style of evangelism?

What are some possible problems with this approach?

10 How can a person with a testimonial style of evangelism develop skills to explain the Gospel more effectively?

11 What kind of people can be reached with this style of evangelism?

*Specifically, who are some people who might respond
to this style of evangelism?*

Note: If you didn't personally relate to any of these styles of
evangelism, hold on. We'll discover three more styles
in the next session.

PUTTING YOURSELF IN THE PICTURE

THINKING ABOUT YOUR FAITH

In 1 Peter 3:15 we read these words: "Always be prepared to
give an answer to everyone who asks you to give the reason
for the hope that you have. But do this with gentleness and
respect." For some people, explaining their faith comes fairly
naturally. For others, it takes more work and effort. Take time
in the coming days to work at preparing yourself to give an
answer for your faith. Prepare yourself to answer these three
questions:

1. Does the Bible really say Jesus is the only way to heaven?
2. Aren't all religions just different paths to God?
3. How do you know the Bible is reliable?

As you think about these questions and develop your ability
to answer them, you will want to use a few resources. A Bible
concordance will be helpful as well as books on apologetics
(defending the faith). You may also want to ask your pastor to
answer these questions for you as part of your study.

TALKING ABOUT YOUR FAITH

Take time in the coming week to practice your testimony.
The best thing you can do is learn to communicate your story
of faith often and to different kinds of people. Try to practice
giving your testimony to a child, a teenager, and an adult. Be
sure your vocabulary makes sense to each person. Also, be
sure to use only terms a seeker would understand. Although
you will most likely be practicing on Christians, you want to
be ready to tell your story of faith to seekers in a way that
makes sense to them.

DISCOVERING YOUR STYLE: PART 2

REFLECTIONS FROM SESSION 5

1. If you took the challenge to think about the questions listed in last week's session, tell your group members how you would respond if a seeker asked one of the following questions:

   • Does the Bible really say Jesus is the only way to heaven?
   • Aren't all religions just different paths to God?
   • How do you know the Bible is reliable?

   How does it feel to have taken time to prepare yourself to respond to some of the questions seekers ask Christians about their faith?

2. If you took time to practice giving your testimony since your last small group session, would you be willing to give it to your small group now? How did telling your testimony to people of various ages help you develop your ability to effectively communicate your story of faith?

THE BIG PICTURE

I have discovered that large numbers of godly people who love Jesus Christ are afraid that if they were to get intentional about spreading the message of Jesus, they would have to become obnoxious. They believe that to become an effective evangelist, they will have to behave in ways that are foreign to how God created them. Therefore, many believers make a silent vow to themselves to just attend church, read their Bible, pray, enjoy fellowship, give some money, and serve in some capacity. They reason that the task of evangelism is better left in the hands of those whose personalities and temperaments are cut out for "that kind of thing." They decide to let outgoing Extroverted Ed spread the Word. To have Dynamic Dave go out and save souls. To leave it to Soapbox Sally to do her thing. "I'll be an usher," they say. "I'll have devotions. I'll help out with the children's choir, because I'm just not cut out to be an evangelist."

This type of thinking is an all-out tragedy for the church. It's a tragedy for lost people. I believe this kind of thinking originated as a satanic scheme to defeat the expansion of the kingdom of God. Sadly, Satan's strategy has been extremely effective. In this session we will confront Satan's scheme and shoot holes in his strategy by discovering three more styles of evangelism.

Don't forget—there are many styles in the ministry of evangelism. In fact, there are as many effective styles in the work of evangelism as there are evangelists. God made you precisely the way He did, in part, so He would have an evangelist just like you to send out into the fields of lost people. There are some seekers who will only be reached by someone just like you.

A WIDE ANGLE VIEW

1 Why do so many followers of Christ fear being an evangelist?

How does a fear of evangelism hurt the kingdom of God and help the kingdom of Satan?

A BIBLICAL PORTRAIT

Read Luke 5:27–32

2 When Matthew became a follower of Christ, one of the first things he did was hold a banquet and invite his friends and fellow tax gatherers into his home. What do you learn from Matthew's evangelism strategy?

How could you mirror this example in your own life?

SHARPENING THE FOCUS

Read Snapshot "Interpersonal Style"

INTERPERSONAL STYLE

When Matthew came to faith, he realized that his tax-collecting friends still didn't know Jesus, so he came up with the idea of throwing a party. I like to call this a "party with a purpose" or a "Matthew Party." It was strategically designed to get his friends to rub shoulders with Jesus and the disciples.

Although all of us need to build relationships with those we hope to reach, those with the interpersonal style specialize in this area. They are able to go deeper relationally with a greater number of people and to become partners with their friends in their journey toward Christ.

3 What are some unique advantages of an interpersonal style of evangelism?

What are some possible problems with this approach?

47

4 How can a person with this style of evangelism develop their ability to explain the Gospel to others?

Read Snapshot "Invitational Style"

INVITATIONAL STYLE

 In John chapter 4 we find the famous story of the woman at the well. In this chapter we see another style of evangelism. Convinced that she had been talking to the Son of God, and rather than try to retell everything in her own words, this woman leaves her water pots and runs into the city to invite people to come hear what Jesus has to say.

Some people are just not as articulate as others. They're not overly confident of themselves and would feel awkward explaining the Gospel to others, but they do feel comfortable inviting a friend to hear someone else teach or sing about Jesus. The woman at the well had a great impact simply because she invited many people to come and hear Jesus.

5 What are some benefits of using an invitational style of evangelism?

What are some possible problems with this approach?

6 How can a person with this style of evangelism develop their ability to explain their faith?

Read Snapshot "Serving Style"

SERVING STYLE

In Acts 9 we read about a woman named Dorcas who had an enormous impact for Christ in her community because of her habit of doing deeds of kindness. Dorcas made garments for the poor and forgotten people in her city and then distributed them in the name of Christ. This is called "service" evangelism. Dorcas served people, and in her service to them, she pointed them to the One who could forgive and transform. She may never have preached a sermon. It's very possible she never knocked on a door. It's quite probable she never passed out literature. But she used her love and service as a vehicle to share the Gospel.

---

7 What are some advantages of a serving style of evangelism?

What are some possible problems with this approach?

8 How can a person with this style of evangelism develop their ability to explain their faith in Jesus Christ?

9 Which of the six styles covered in sessions five and six best fits you and why?

What can you do to develop this approach to evangelism?

PUTTING YOURSELF IN THE PICTURE

Planning a "Matthew Party"

As you finish this study on becoming stronger salt and brighter light, put your faith into action using what you have learned. Plan a party, BBQ, or dinner for your small group members and have everyone invite one seeker friend or couple. Pray for this opportunity for your Christian friends to have an impact on those seekers.

LEADER'S NOTES

Leading a Bible discussion—especially for the first time—can make you feel both nervous and excited. If you are nervous, realize that you are in good company. Many biblical leaders, such as Moses, Joshua, and the apostle Paul, felt nervous and inadequate to lead others (see, for example, 1 Corinthians 2:3). Yet God's grace was sufficient for them, just as it will be for you.

Some excitement is also natural. Your leadership is a gift to the others in the group. Keep in mind, however, that other group members also share responsibility for the group. Your role is simply to stimulate discussion by asking questions and encouraging people to respond. The suggestions listed below can help you to be an effective leader.

PREPARING TO LEAD

1. Ask God to help you understand and apply the passage to your own life. Unless that happens, you will not be prepared to lead others.
2. Carefully work through each question in the study guide. Meditate and reflect on the passage as you formulate your answers.
3. Familiarize yourself with the leader's notes for each session. These will help you understand the purpose of the session and will provide valuable information about the questions in the session.
4. Pray for the various members of the group. Ask God to use these sessions to make you better disciples of Jesus Christ.
5. Before the first session, make sure each person has a study guide. Encourage them to prepare beforehand for each session.

LEADING THE SESSION

1. Begin the session on time. If people realize that the session begins on schedule, they will work harder to arrive on time.
2. At the beginning of your first time together, explain that these sessions are designed to be discussions, not lectures. Encourage everyone to participate, but realize some may be hesitant to speak during the first few sessions.

3. Don't be afraid of silence. People in the group may need time to think before responding.
4. Avoid answering your own questions. If necessary, rephrase a question until it is clearly understood. Even an eager group will quickly become passive and silent if they think the leader will do most of the talking.
5. Encourage more than one answer to each question. Ask, "What do the rest of you think?" or "Anyone else?" until several people have had a chance to respond.
6. Try to be affirming whenever possible. Let people know you appreciate their insights into the passage.
7. Never reject an answer. If it is clearly wrong, ask, "Which verse led you to that conclusion?" Or let the group handle the problem by asking them what they think about the question.
8. Avoid going off on tangents. If people wander off course, gently bring them back to the passage being considered.
9. Conclude your time together with conversational prayer. Ask God to help you apply those things that you learned in the session.
10. End on time. This will be easier if you control the pace of the discussion by not spending too much time on some questions or too little on others.

We encourage all small group leaders to use *Leading Life-Changing Small Groups* (Zondervan) by Bill Donahue while leading their group. Developed and used by Willow Creek Community Church, this guide is an excellent resource for training and equipping followers of Christ to effectively lead small groups. It includes valuable information on how to utilize fun and creative relationship-building exercises for your group; how to plan your meeting; how to share the leadership load by identifying, developing, and working with an "apprentice leader;" and how to find creative ways to do group prayer. In addition, the book includes material and tips on handling potential conflicts and difficult personalities, forming group covenants, inviting new members, improving listening skills, studying the Bible, and much more. Using *Leading Life-Changing Small Groups* will help you create a group that members love to be a part of.

Now let's discuss the different elements of this small group study guide and how to use them for the session portion of your group meeting.

THE BIG PICTURE

Each session will begin with a short story or overview of the central theme called "The Big Picture." You will need to read this section as a group or have group members read it on their own before discussion begins. Here are three ways you can approach this section of the small group session:

- As the group leader, read this section out loud for the whole group and then move into the questions in the next section, "A Wide Angle View." (You might read the first week, but then use the other two options below to encourage group involvement.)
- Ask a group member to volunteer to read this section for the group. This allows another group member to participate. It is best to ask someone in advance to give them time to read over the section before reading it to the group. It is also good to ask someone to volunteer and not to assign this task. Some people do not feel comfortable reading in front of a group. After a group member has read this section out loud, move into the discussion questions.
- Allow time at the beginning of the group for each person to read this section silently. If you do this, be sure to allow enough time for everyone to finish reading so they can think about what they've read and be ready for meaningful discussion.

A WIDE ANGLE VIEW

This section includes one or more questions that move the group into a general discussion of the session topic. These questions are designed to help group members begin discussing the topic in an open and honest manner. Once the topic of the session has been established, move on to the Bible passage for the session.

A BIBLICAL PORTRAIT

This portion of the session includes a Scripture reading and one or more questions that help group members see how the theme of the session is rooted and based in biblical teaching. The Scripture reading can be handled just like "The Big Picture" section: You can read it for the group, have a group member read it, or allow time for silent reading. Make sure everyone has a Bible or that you have Bibles available for those who need them. Once you have read the passage, ask the question(s) in this section so that group members can dig into the truth of the Bible.

SHARPENING THE FOCUS

The majority of the discussion questions for the session are in this section. These questions are practical and help group members apply biblical teaching to their daily lives.

SNAPSHOTS

The "Snapshots" in each session help prepare group members for discussion. These anecdotes give additional insight to the topic being discussed. Each "Snapshot" should be read at a designated point in the session. This is clearly marked in the session as well as in the leader's notes. Again, follow the same format as you do with "The Big Picture" section and the "Biblical Portrait" section: Either you read the anecdote, have a group member volunteer to read, or provide time for silent reading. However you approach this section, you will find these anecdotes very helpful in triggering lively dialogue and moving discussion in a meaningful direction.

PUTTING YOURSELF IN THE PICTURE

Here's where you roll up your sleeves and put the truth into action. This portion is very practical and action-oriented. At the end of each session there will be suggestions for one or two ways group members can put what they've just learned into practice. Review the action goals at the end of each session and challenge group members to work on one or more of them in the coming week.

You will find follow-up questions for the "Putting Yourself in the Picture" section at the beginning of the next week's session. Starting with the second week, there will be time set aside at the beginning of the session to look back and talk about how you have tried to apply God's Word in your life since your last time together.

PRAYER

You will want to open and close your small group with a time of prayer. Occasionally, there will be specific direction within a session for how you can do this. Most of the time, however, you will need to decide the best place to stop and pray. You may want to pray or have a group member volunteer to begin the session with a prayer. Or you might want to read "The Big Picture" and discuss the "Wide Angle View" questions before opening in prayer. In some cases, it might be best to open in prayer after you have read the Bible passage. You need to decide where you feel an opening prayer best fits for your group.

When opening in prayer, think in terms of the session theme and pray for group members (including yourself) to be responsive to the truth of Scripture and the working of the

Holy Spirit. If you have seekers in your group (people investigating Christianity but not yet believers) be sensitive to your expectations for group prayer. Seekers may not yet be ready to take part in group prayer.

Be sure to close your group with a time of prayer as well. One option is for you to pray for the entire group. Or you might allow time for group members to offer audible prayers that others can agree with in their hearts. Another approach would be to allow a time of silence for one-on-one prayers with God and then to close this time with a simple "Amen."

BEING SALT AND LIGHT

Matthew 5:13–16

INTRODUCTION

As we begin this study on evangelism, the members of any small group will have mixed feelings. If you have not done so already, take a moment and read the introduction to this study guide. It addresses some possible responses group members may have to this topic. Those who are reluctant or fearful need a clear word of encouragement as you begin. They need to know they will not be pressured or embarrassed along the way. They need a word of affirmation that God wants to use them as salt and light just the way they are. Assure them that they will not be pressured, manipulated, or made to feel guilty. The key will be for each of them to learn how to identify their personal evangelism style. The goal of this study is to help them develop their personal evangelism skills in a way that is natural and comfortable.

THE BIG PICTURE

Take time to read this introduction with the group. There are suggestions for how this can be done in the beginning of this leader's section.

A WIDE ANGLE VIEW

Question One Think about salt for a moment and why Jesus chose to use salt as a metaphor for how we should go out and affect the world. What does salt do? One obvious answer is that it makes you thirsty. Isn't that why salty food is widely served in bars? Bar owners want people to eat salty pretzels, peanuts, and popcorn so they will drink more beverages. Salt makes people thirsty.

Salt also spices things up a bit; it enhances flavor. Can you imagine corn on the cob without salt? It would be bland without a dash of salt to bring out the flavor.

Salt also preserves. People knew this long before the days of the refrigerator. Salt was used to keep certain foods from spoiling. If packed in salt, these foods could be preserved for long periods of time.

Salt creates thirst, enhances flavor, and preserves. This leads us to the big question: What *specifically* did Jesus have in mind when He looked at His followers and said, "You are the salt of the earth." We don't know for certain. Maybe Jesus meant for the metaphor of salt to symbolize all three. The key is, salt makes a positive difference.

Light illuminates dark places and helps us see where we need to go. It takes away fear and allows us to move ahead with confidence. Christians are called to be light in this world of darkness. When the radiance of Jesus fills our lives, we naturally reflect this light in the way we live and in the words we speak. As God's lightbearers, we are called to make sure nothing keeps His light from shining in our lives.

A BIBLICAL PORTRAIT

Read Matthew 5:13–16

Question Two The call to be like light and salt is found in many passages in the Bible. For instance, in Acts 1:8 Jesus is about ready to ascend to the Father. Before He leaves, He looks at His followers and says, in effect, "You are appointed from this day on to be My witnesses. And I want you to go out under the anointing power of the Holy Spirit and be powerful, Spirit-anointed witnesses." He wanted them to make an impact on their world.

In 2 Corinthians 5:18–19 Paul tells us that we are given the challenge of being ministers of reconciliation. We're trying to reconcile lost men and women to God through what Jesus did on the cross. And we ought to be serious about this responsibility.

In the Great Commission found in Matthew 28:19–20, Jesus sends His followers to the four corners of the earth. He wants every Christian to reach out with the Gospel, to lead people to faith, to have maximum impact, to be fishers of men. In other words, Christians are called to be salt and light wherever we go—and that's everywhere!

This kind of a lifestyle creates a thirst in others. Likewise, when Christ's followers are bold and innovative in their witness for Christ in the world, they spice up things, don't they? I mean, they put a little zing in a bland world. They upset some apple carts. They make people think and reconsider their values and beliefs.

By living a Christ-honoring life, believers tend to retard the moral decay in the society in which they live. As light, we illuminate those things that try to hide in the darkness. When fully devoted followers of Christ shine the light of their Savior, the darkness begins to disappear.

Sharpening the Focus

Read Snapshot "An Equation for Evangelism: (HP + CP + CC = MI)" before Question 3

Question Three In Matthew 5:13 Jesus says that salt that has lost its punch is worthless—it can have little or no impact. Flavorless salt, you see, won't create much thirst. It won't add much spice or retard much moral decay. It can have all kinds of proximity, but if it lacks potency, it is virtually worthless. By the same token, salty salt—industrial-strength salt—has all the impact potential in the world, but it won't actualize that potential unless it gets near that which it is attempting to affect. The key is for us to increase our saltiness as well as our proximity to seekers.

In the same way, light can be dim or bright. We are called to increase our brightness as we live in God's presence and speak His truth. The best way to increase potency is to spend time with Jesus. As His followers, we need to walk in His footsteps. This means we need to study God's Word, talk to Jesus in prayer, worship God in Spirit and in truth, and serve Him with joy in our hearts. If we do these things, our potency level will go off the scale.

Question Four Becky Pippert made a great observation some years ago when she wrote her classic book *Out of the Salt Shaker and Into the World*. She said, "Unless the salt gets shaken out of the salt shaker and onto something, it remains a mere table ornament." This is a fairly good description of a number of Christians. They may have high potency, but they are still in the salt shaker. They are never rubbing up against the people they need to affect, so their lives remain powerful but ineffective. In the same way, their light may be bright, but it is hidden under a bowl. They need to get their light up on a stand so everyone can see it.

As we try to increase our proximity with seekers, we need to look at the natural contacts we have. Most people have more contact with seekers than they realize. Think through your daily routine and identify those people in your workplace, neighborhood, or family with whom you have contact on a regular basis. Where do you buy gas or coffee in the morning? Where do you grocery shop or exercise? What clubs, recreational pursuits, or social groups do you attend? If you have children, what contacts do you have through their school or sporting events? The possible points of contact are countless. The key is for Christians to identify these opportunities and seek to be salt and light wherever we go. We also need to intentionally find new points of contact so we can be continuously increasing our proximity to seekers.

How's your proximity factor? One of my favorite stories in the Bible is found in Luke 5:27–32. After Matthew is converted, this transformed tax collector throws a party and invites Jesus and the disciples to come. Matthew sees that Jesus and the disciples are plenty salty. Then he invites all of his tax-gathering friends who need to come to faith. He is hoping that as Jesus and the disciples are in close proximity rubbing shoulders with his irreligious friends some spiritual sparks will fly.

Question Five This could be a tender and vulnerable question; however, it is an important one. Each member of your group needs to recognize where they are in this equation. Only when they are honest about this question can they move on and grow in their effectiveness as salt and light.

All components of the equation have to be active for maximum impact to be achieved. Does the equation accurately reflect the condition of your life with regard to trying to influence seekers? Are you getting up close to seekers on a regular basis? Is your spiritual life potent enough to make an impact when you are near seekers? Are you able to communicate the message of Jesus with clarity? Are you regularly having maximum influence on those outside of God's family?

Question Six *Spiritual confidence*—A person making an impact for Christ is often a person with spiritual confidence. This believer is sure of his or her salvation. If she can't give you the exact date and time she became a Christian, she can at least narrow it down to an era. She looks you right in the eye and says, "I was lost. Now I'm found. I was an alien. Now I am a citizen. I was a stranger. Now I am a daughter."

Part of this confidence is based on having enough biblical knowledge to feel strong and secure in the truth of God's Word. They have read enough and discussed their faith enough to have confidence in their ability to answer tough questions frequently asked about Christianity. These people have had a relationship with Christ long enough to know that He is faithful—even in the valleys and snares of life.

An authentic faith—Christians who have maximum impact are spiritually authentic. There is a sincerity factor about them. They seem renewed. Their relationship with Christ seems genuine and personal. They are humble. They talk about their relationship with Jesus like they would talk about a relationship with a close friend. When they pray, you can tell they are genuine. They admit when they are wrong. They have an accepting spirit. They listen without judging. They say, "I don't know," when they don't know. They are eager to learn and grow. This authenticity makes them contagious.

An urgency about the Gospel—Followers of Christ whose lights shine brightly have a sense of urgency about them. They walk with purpose in their step. They have figured out what's important in life and what's not so important, and they stay focused on that which really matters. They are most concerned about people because they have learned that people matter to God. They have tuned into what the Holy Spirit is doing in their lives and in the world and are serious and urgent about being obedient to the Spirit's leading.

People with an urgency about the Gospel find a way to focus on the eternal in the midst of the temporal things of the world. They live with an ear open to heaven and an eye on eternity. While everyone else is trudging through daily routines, they try to see what God might make of a conversation or relationship. They think a lot about eternity—about heaven and hell and the day of reckoning. There's an urgency about their desire to influence others with the time that remains in their lives. Every day and moment is precious and valuable.

Read Snapshot "Spiritual Disciplines" before Question 7

Questions Seven & Eight We need to start asking each other, "How is your Bible reading going lately?" There needs to be a time in your holy place where you get God's Book out and say, "I need to be fed from God's Word today." Almost every major change in life comes as a direct result of being influenced by the truth in His Book.

How's your prayer time? How's your serving? Are you doing the things that must be done to make your walk with Jesus intimate, personal, and powerful? How's the depth and the quality of your fellowship? Are you close enough to some brothers and sisters so that when your embers get a little cold, you can turn to someone around you and get next to their embers so you can catch fire again? In the same way, when someone else gets a little cold, do your hot embers warm them up a little bit?

We all need to focus on the basics. We must be committed to fellowship, communion, serving, giving, and to sharing our faith when Christ gives an open door. Combining the sustained discipline of Bible reading and prayer with the corporate experience of spiritual worship keeps our lives potent, our savor factors high, our lights shining.

Question Nine Take time to allow group members to communicate the changes that need to be made in their lives. Discuss the core elements of spiritual growth they feel need to be rediscovered in their lives. It will be helpful for you, as the group leader, to begin the discussion by talking about an area where you desire to grow in *your* spiritual life. Then, allow time for group members to interact honestly with each other.

PUTTING YOURSELF IN THE PICTURE

Let the group members know you will be providing time at the beginning of the next session for them to discuss how they have put their faith into action. Let them tell about how they have acted on one of the two options listed for this section. However, don't limit their interaction to these two options. They may have put themselves into the picture in some other way. Allow for honest and open communication.

Also, be clear that there will not be any kind of a "test" or forced reporting. All you are going to do is allow time for people to volunteer to talk about how they have applied what they learned in your last session. Some group members will feel pressured if they think you are going to make everyone report on how they acted on these action goals. You don't want anyone to skip the next session because they are afraid of having to say they did not follow up on what they learned from the prior session. The key is to provide a place for honest communication without creating pressure or fear of embarrassment.

Every session from this point on will open with a look back at the "Putting Yourself in the Picture" section of the previous session.

THE MOTIVATION FOR EVANGELISM

Acts 1:6–8

INTRODUCTION

What moves followers of Christ to share their faith with others? What helps us get beyond ourselves to actually reach out to a seeker? What inspires Christians to move out of their comfort zone so they can be light in the darkness and salt in a world that needs to thirst for Christ?

This session give four powerful motivations for evangelism. As you prepare to lead this session, pray for the Holy Spirit to move in the heart of each group member. Pray for motivation and inspiration to be salt and light in a flavorless and dark world.

THE BIG PICTURE

Take time to read this introduction with the group. There are suggestions for how this can be done in the beginning of this leader's section.

A WIDE ANGLE VIEW

Questions One & Two Be sure this discussion does not center only on the actual act of telling the Gospel story. People convey their faith through testimony, friendship, example, an invitation to church, and countless other ways. Encourage group members to tell some of their stories of how faith has been imparted.

The second part of these questions is a little tougher than the first. We don't often identify motives, nor do we speak of our motivations very freely. Allow time for group members to identify their motives as well as the motives of others. Don't limit discussion to the four motivations discussed in this session; allow for open communication of *any* motives—you may discover some that don't come up in the session but are very real to your group members.

A BIBLICAL PORTRAIT

Read Acts 1:6–8

Question Three Like it or not, we are God's witnesses. Each and every follower of Christ is called to bring the message of salvation to the ends of the earth. Some will resist the idea that they are a central part in God's plan of reconciliation. Others will willingly and zealously accept it. In either case, encourage honest discussion among your group members.

SHARPENING THE FOCUS

Read Snapshot "The Stockpile Factor"
before Question 4

Question Four A major theme of my teaching ministry over the years has been the character of God and the identity of the believer. When we watch people who matter to God go from bar to bar, toy to toy, fun fix to fun fix, lover to lover, fad to fad, we realize they need the message of Jesus Christ to fill their emptiness. As we grow in our understanding of what God has given us, it compels us to let some of our stockpile overflow to those who are starving for what we have.

The more I walk with Christ, the less I feel compelled to point accusing fingers at people who are rebelling against God. Instead, I just feel sad for them. I feel a kind of pity I never used to feel. I find myself saying to them, "Taste and see that the Lord is good. He is better than whatever you are trying to replace Him with." I feel like telling every scavenger I meet, "Stop picking at the refuse piles; there is a stockpile in the kingdom of God. There is plenty of God's grace, there is plenty of His favor, there is plenty of His love, if you will only accept it."

One of the best forms of motivation for personal evangelism is to have a sense of wonder about your spiritual stockpile. Protect it, work on it, thank God for it, and share it with others.

Read Snapshot "A Heavenly Honor" before Question 5

Question Five Every single believer is called to be exactly who God created him or her to be. You are called to be God's spokesperson with your personality, gifts, talents, abilities, and your particular perspective on life. You are called to speak on behalf of God, to reach out to lost people who matter to Him. Those people need a person just like you. You are central to God's plan in your workplace, at your health club, on the street where you live, and everywhere you go.

I find this to be very motivational. Someday, I want to stand before God and hear Him say to me, "Well done, you good and faithful ambassador; well done, you good and faithful agent of Mine. You know, I carved out a space for you on the planet, I carved out a neighborhood, I carved out a group of people who desperately needed you. They needed your life, they needed your personality, they needed your witness, they needed your age factor, they needed your sense of humor, they needed you, and you were faithful!"

I find it enormously motivating to go through my day trying to figure out what serendipitous kind of occasion is going to surface in which I can be used by God as a spokesperson for His kingdom. I try to pray every single day, "Lord, I don't know where You are going to put me today, what opportunities You are going to orchestrate for me to tell some lost person that they matter. I don't know what You have in mind today, but God, I want to be a part of it. I really do." We need to get excited about how God can use us. We need to look for the opportunities God sends our way.

Question Six Jesus said, "You are going to receive power. The Holy Spirit is going to come upon you, and His presence will help you to become effective witnesses." When we are humble, pure, and in tune with the Holy Spirit, when we are living with a spirit of anticipation about being spirit-filled agents, and when we are asking to be used by the Holy Spirit, we will have many opportunities to be witnesses. When we are a little off base spiritually, not so tuned into the Holy Spirit, grinding out our agenda and saying, "Lord, I'm not all that concerned with what You have for me today because I'm overwhelmed by what I have to do," we can find ourselves going for weeks at a time without having any opportunities to be a spokesperson for the kingdom. We need the leading and the power of the Holy Spirit if we are to be effective ambassadors for Christ.

Read Snapshot "The Reality of Hell" before Question 7

Question Seven Jesus grieved when the rich young ruler refused to receive spiritual wealth in exchange for temporal wealth, because He knew the man was walking down the road that led to hell. Jesus felt sorrow over the city of Jerusalem, because He said He could see them as sheep wandering around without a shepherd, and that it was only a matter of time before they would go off the cliffs of eternity into the abyss of hell forever. Jesus confronted anybody and everybody with the basic message that unless they turned and put their faith in Him, they would die in their sins and face condemnation in eternity.

Why did Jesus keep the pace He did, teaching from early morning until late night? Why did He endure ridicule day in and day out? Because He knew people were on the road headed toward hell. It broke His heart, and it motivated His witness.

If you have time, you may want to read Luke 16:19–31 as a group. It's the parable of the rich man who lived in splendor while a poor man named Lazarus was starving to death at his gate. Eventually, they both died. The poor man, Lazarus, had known about matters pertaining to salvation and went to heaven, while the rich man ended up in hell. In verse 24, we read of the rich man's desire for Lazarus to bring him a drop of cool water. When this is refused, he appeals for Lazarus to go to his family and warn them about the torments of hell. Five minutes in hell turned the unbelieving rich man into an evangelist. He was finally motivated. He pleaded for someone to go and warn his brothers that hell is real. If only we could gain that perspective, what a motivation it would be!

Part of the reason I am as serious about the things of God as I am, and part of the reason why I do the work of an evangelist, is because I believe in hell. I really do. I believe in it consciously, and I believe in it emotionally. I am not neurotic about it, but I'll tell you what, it impacts me every day. The apostle Paul knew that if there is no heaven or hell, our faith is a lie. Just read 1 Corinthians 15—it's clear as can be. If there is no hell, then why all the time spent in service around the church? Why all the energy? Why all the giving, praying, and pleading with people? Why all the work? Why would followers of Christ pour so much time into reaching out to seekers?

Like Paul, we know the resurrection is real. We know every person we come into contact with will either spend eternity in heaven or a Christless eternity in hell. This hard reality should put a passion in our hearts and a fire in our souls. We are His light and salt, so let's start acting like it! Eternity weighs in the balance.

Read Snapshot "The Joy of Salvation" before Question 8

Question Eight Some of your group members will have very engaging stories to tell that recapture the joy of a sinner coming to Christ. Others may not be able to identify with the feeling of being used by God to reach a seeker with the Gospel. This is not a time to heap guilt on someone because they have never led someone to Christ. Simply focus on the stories of victory and pray for them to be an inspiration to others.

PUTTING YOURSELF IN THE PICTURE

Challenge group members to take time in the coming week to use part or all of this application section as an opportunity for continued growth.

THE EVANGELIST'S MIND-SET

Matthew 4:18–20

INTRODUCTION

This study focuses on what should be central in the heart and mind of an evangelist. If we are in the evangelism business, we are in the people business. We must realize that people matter to God. If we have the heart of God, people will also matter to us as well.

Like Peter and Andrew, most of us have some kind of vocational pursuit in our lives. We all have some passion or focus that draws much of our time and resources. For Peter and Andrew it was fishing. For us it might be our jobs, education, personal goals, or a number of other things. Jesus asked two fishermen to change the central focus of their lives. He called them to set aside their fishing nets and become fishers of men. This same invitation is given to us today. What needs to be set aside in our lives so that we can effectively reach out to seekers with the Good News of Jesus Christ?

THE BIG PICTURE

Take time to read this introduction with the group. There are suggestions for how this can be done in the beginning of this leader's section.

A BIBLICAL PORTRAIT

Read Matthew 4:18–20

Question Three Dig deep on this question. There are some obvious similarities and differences between fishermen and fishers of men. However, when you move beyond the obvious, you will find some similarities that will surprise you. Allow enough time on this question for group members to reflect and interact more deeply.

SHARPENING THE FOCUS

Read Snapshot "The People Business" before Question 5

Question Five I can tell you exactly where I was sitting when it happened to me. I was in a chair in the sales office of Hybels' Produce Company in Kalamazoo, Michigan. I was working in the marketplace and loving being there. I was having my private devotions when I read 2 Peter 3:10, and it just wiped me out. The verse simply says, "There is coming a time when every single thing on this planet will melt with a fervent heat. It will all be consumed." And I thought, "Here I am, totally preoccupied with selling produce and using the money I earn from selling produce to buy toys that make me happy." I was a Christian totally preoccupied with fishing instead of being a fisher of men.

It hit me like a lightening bolt: "Every single thing I'm working for is going to go up in smoke. The only thing that lasts for eternity is people. So what am I doing being preoccupied with all of this stuff that is going to burn up? Why am I not preoccupied with people?"

I started thinking, "I ought to go around and put a little red tag that says '**Temporal, Temporal, Temporal**' in bold letters on every thing that seems so important now. Then I should go around and put a green tag that says, **'Eternal, Eternal, Eternal**' on every person in my life." I realized I needed a whole new perspective on life.

I also thought of the passage in 1 Corinthians 9:24–27 where the apostle Paul says, "You know, there are some people who will knock themselves out, train, practice, and discipline themselves for a perishable wreath that will wither and fade in a matter of weeks." He says, "They are all cranked up about the wrong race. I would rather all you believers train and practice and set your sights on winning the real race—the race of making your life count for eternity." How do we make our lives really count? By serving God and serving people!

I realize only a few of us will actually be asked to leave our nets, only a few will be asked to abandon our professions, only a few will hear God call us into vocational ministry. The vast majority of Jesus' followers will simply be asked to function in this life with a whole new mind-set—a mind-set that reflects God's attitudes and perspectives, that affirms the eternal importance of the people business. There is more to life than setting new fishing records at the fish market every single day. There is more to life than buying more nets and out-fitting more boats and building bigger carts to carry more fish to market. What good is a life totally devoted to setting fishing records? What will there be in eternity to show for a preoccupation with fish?

Jesus is trying to teach all of us to work hard at whatever business we have been gifted to build and maintain. But we must always remember that bringing people to Christ is a higher calling. When the two go head-to-head, as they inevitably will, Jesus says, "Major in the people business and minor in fish." There will be greater rewards in this life and in eternity for being fishers of men.

Read Snapshot "What Sets Us Apart?"
before Question 6

Question Six As I spoke with that Christian businessman, I shared a few words in response to his questions. I said to him, "Does a moral humanitarian care about a man's soul? Does a moral humanitarian care about whether or not a human being ends up in hell? Does a moral humanitarian weep at night because not enough people are worshiping the Savior? Does a moral humanitarian get a lump in his throat when he sees people walking around picking at the refuse heaps in life, looking for meaning? No! They may be caring, but they are not concerned about eternal things."

I continued, "It seems to me that you ought to be doing more than just selling cars. You ought to be doing more than catching fish. You ought to be a fisher of men and women."

Before he left the conference, the man said to me, "I'm going to make a difference. I'm going to do more than sell cars. I'm going to try to reach into the souls of my people and point them to Christ. That will set me apart from the moral humanitarian, won't it?"

What makes us Christians different? Shouldn't it be that deep down we have a yearning and a longing for lost people to be rightly related with the risen Christ? Shouldn't we be taking every imaginable step to present Christ to lost people? Jesus wants you and me to believe in the core of our being that it is infinitely more important to catch men and women for Christ than it is to catch fish.

Question Seven This is a lot of Scripture—read these ahead of time and select some key verses to discuss as a group. Use the information below as a guide.

From the beginning of Jesus' ministry all the way to the end, He taught that men and women matter more than fish:

Luke 4:14–21—Jesus came to His hometown of Nazareth, entered the synagogue on the Sabbath, and stood up to read from Isaiah. This was sort of Jesus' inaugural statement. He said, "I want all of you to know why I'm here on this earth. I'm not here to build an earthly kingdom or to set up a commercial carpentry business. I'm here because I'm in the people business. My agenda is preaching and reaching and serving people." Can you see the passion of Jesus' heart in this passage?

Luke 14:12–14—In this passage, Jesus clarifies what kind of people really matter to God. He doesn't want there to be any confusion. He says, "I'm in the people business, and all of my followers should be in the people business." What kind of people was He referring to? Jesus says in this text, "The forgotten people. The poor, crippled, lame, and blind." He wants us to be in the business of reaching out, touching, serving, loving, affirming, and building up those who are forgotten and downtrodden.

Luke 15—In an effort to help the skeptical religious leaders understand His love and concern for people, Jesus told stories about a lost sheep, a lost coin, and a prodigal son. In each of these stories, something of great value winds up missing. Also in each of these stories, that which is missing matters so much that someone searches for it or anxiously awaits its return. When each is found, there is celebration and great rejoicing. The bottom line to all three stories is the powerful lesson, "In the same way that these people celebrate finding something lost, I tell you there is joy in the presence of the angels of God over one sinner who repents." God cares about people. Even one lost person who is found warrants a heavenly party. You better believe people matter to God.

Luke 19:1–10—In this story of Zacchaeus we again see Jesus' deep concern for people. Jesus is showing us that He is not only in the poor people business, the forgotten people business, and the wayward people business, but He is in the rich people business too. Jesus was interested in reaching the up-and-outers every bit as much as the down-and-outers, because net worth in earthly terms doesn't really matter; *people* matter.

The church should be preoccupied with the business of reaching, serving, encouraging, teaching, training, admonishing, loving, and counseling people. When we stay in the people business, we can anticipate the full blessing of God. When we get into the entertainment business or any other kind of business, we can fully expect the removal of God's blessing from our churches. No matter what we are doing, we must keep asking the question, "Will what we are doing here really reach lost people?"

Question Eight Needless to say, it is a tough, tough job to change a fisherman into a fisher of men. Take a guy like Peter. For all of these years he had been preoccupied with setting fishing records. For all of his life, the people he had employed were simply a means to that end. Professional fishermen needed people to carry and clean nets, and to carry fish to the market. If the workers performed, they were paid; if they didn't, they were fired. Now, all of a sudden, Peter is being asked to follow Jesus and experience a whole new mind-set.

Suddenly, people who were mere employees to him were transformed into beings of supreme importance to the Savior, and therefore, supreme importance to the Christian. Peter needed to be concerned with their eternal destiny, not just their daily job description. Those net carriers mattered to God.

All of this was foreign to Peter, and it's foreign to most of us as well. It's mind-boggling. Changing a mind-set in a capitalistic society is tough business. Transforming a fisherman into a fisher of men is a full-time job for the Holy Spirit. Believe me. He is trying to do that work of transformation in me and in you.

As a group, think of practical ways you can reach out to those who do not presently follow Christ. What can you do to keep your focus on fishing for people?

Closing

You may want to use this as a closing prayer for your group:

Lord, we live in a competitive world. Everywhere we look, everything we read, every time we turn on the television set, we hear the voice of the world saying, "The one with the most toys wins. The ones with the money, the big house, the new clothes, and the expensive trips are the successful people." Without even knowing it and without meaning to harm You, we have gotten caught up in setting fishing records. We confess that sometimes we focus more on fishing than on the people who matter to You. Holy Spirit, speak to us this day. Let us know that it's fine to fish, but help us never to major on it. Instead, help us to major on bringing men and women to the Cross. May we live with a holy discomfort when we focus only on fish, and an enormous surge of encouragement when we faithfully seek to be fishers of people. For Jesus' sake, amen.

PUTTING YOURSELF IN THE PICTURE

Challenge group members to take time in the coming week to use part or all of this application section as an opportunity for continued growth.

THE EVANGELIST'S MESSAGE

Acts 2:14–41

INTRODUCTION

The message of an evangelist has the power to transform human lives. Just before Jesus' ascension He said, "I want you to take my message all over the world. Don't stop spreading the message until everyone in the world has heard it." Paul said in Romans 1:16, "I am not ashamed of the Gospel." He said, "The power of God brings salvation into the lives of men and women. It's a powerful message. It transforms lives. Never shrink back from declaring it whenever you have the opportunity."

Paul also said in 1 Corinthians that people must hear and understand the message of Christ before they can make a decision about it. Our job is to communicate the message so people can reason it through and make a decision about Jesus. Since the days of the early church, tens of thousands of believers just like you and me have been ridiculed, beaten, tortured, imprisoned, and killed for spreading the message. Still they suffered and gave all they had because they wanted to obey the call of Jesus to "spread the Gospel all over the world." They felt like Paul when he said, "I am not apologizing one minute. I'm not shrinking back. It's a powerful, life-changing message." Our call is to communicate this same Gospel today. We are the next generation of those called to share the message of Jesus with a lost people who matter to God.

THE BIG PICTURE

Take time to read this introduction with the group. There are suggestions for how this can be done in the beginning of this leader's section.

A WIDE ANGLE VIEW

Question One The responses to this question can vary from the excitement of getting news about a pregnancy to the anxiety of awaiting the results of a test for cancer. This discussion will help group members get to know a little more about others in the group. The key is to focus on the sense of anticipation in the waiting process. What moment in life is more critical than the moment a person seeks answers to questions of their eternal destiny?

A BIBLICAL PORTRAIT

Read Acts 2:14–41

This passage is longer than other readings in this study guide. However, the story line is very important. You may want to read Question 2 before the passage so your group members can know what to look for during the Scripture reading.

Question Two In Acts 2 we have some high drama. The Holy Spirit has just come in power upon the disciples. After being filled with the Holy Spirit and given the supernatural capacity to communicate the message of Christ in foreign languages, the disciples start witnessing boldly. The crowd is confused by these common men speaking in various languages, but they are also amazed as they hear the disciples praising the wonderful works of God. In the midst of all this, Peter stands up in front of thousands of people and begins declaring the message of salvation.

As Peter preached, he explained the life, death, and resurrection of Jesus Christ. He told the crowd, "You murdered God's Son. You didn't think Jesus was the Messiah, but He was. And He proved it when He came back to life. You murdered the wrong man. You should have repented and submitted to Him." He preached with power, passion, and a persuasiveness only the Holy Spirit could supply.

When he concluded his message, the whole multitude was pierced to the heart. They said to Peter and the rest of the disciples, "Brothers, what shall we do?"

Think of the drama of this moment. Here's a whole multitude of people suddenly aware of their sinfulness. They have realized the horrible mistake they made, and they want to be made right with God. They begin crying out, "Help us, Peter, help us. Tell us, how do sinful people get right with God?

What must we do?" That's high drama. Over three thousand people that day became followers of Jesus.

Question Three The words Peter spoke to the crowd meant the difference between an eternity in heaven with God or a Christless existence in hell. His words at that critical moment were far more important than any verdict a judge or jury could ever pronounce. Peter's words had eternal significance!

Peter had listened to Jesus' teaching for three years. He had heard Jesus say, "I am the way, the truth, and the life. No man will ever be made right with the Father, except through Me." Peter knew how sinners could be made right with the holy God. Only by receiving the gift of grace, forgiveness, and salvation through the death, burial, and resurrection of Jesus Christ could this multitude have any hope for eternity.

With boldness and clarity, Peter presented the crowd with the core of the Gospel message. He said to all of them, "You're going to have to *repent*! You're going to have to assume responsibility for the sins you've committed. You're going to have to change your mind about the way you've been living and agree with God that the path you've been on is the wrong path. You're going to have to repent."

Next, Peter said, "You're going to have to *receive forgiveness* through Jesus Christ, and then be baptized as a public demonstration that you mean business." And then he said, "You're going to receive the gift of the *Holy Spirit,* and He will help you grow and change."

Three thousand people repented, received forgiveness through Christ, and received the gift of the Holy Spirit who began the work of transformation. Pentecost Day—what a day that was! The New Testament church was born. What a drama! What a powerful message! What a work of God to transform three thousand lives just like that! And what a messenger Peter was, to preach the whole Gospel with no compromise.

SHARPENING THE FOCUS

**Read Snapshot "A Personal Testimony"
before Question 4**

Question Four Having members of the group share their testimonies may take quite a bit of time. You might want to limit this question to three or four testimonies.

Here is a brief example of what a testimony might look like. You may want to read this for your group:

Your friend at work is named John. You've been spending time with him for some time now. You've established a friendship. You've been praying for him. He thinks he's a Christian—you know he's not. So, over lunch one day, you feel an opening coming from the Holy Spirit and you say something like this, "John, for the first thirty-two years of my life I thought I was a Christian, but I really wasn't. I thought I was a Christian because I had a spiritual heritage. I was baptized. I even went through confirmation. I attended church once in a while, and I tried to lead a moral life. A few years back, I found out what a real Christian is, and I became one. If you'd ever be interested in hearing how I became one, I'd be happy to explain it to you. Because becoming a Christian has been the best decision of my life."

In the case of many people in your group, this may be an honest testimony they could communicate to a seeker. A personal testimony is a nonthreatening, nonaccusatory, nonpreachy telling of your story. All you're trying to do is get a seeker to think. When John hears somebody he respects say, "I thought I was a Christian, but found out I wasn't," he starts thinking. Also notice that you leave the ball in his court: "If you'd ever be interested in hearing how I became a Christian, I'd be happy to tell you about it." If John says, "Well, I'm not very interested," fine. Order lunch, talk about the family, discuss current events, don't push it. Allow the Holy Spirit to work in his heart and keep praying and looking for the next natural opportunity to discuss spiritual things. If he is open and ready, be prepared to share the Gospel of Jesus.

When you begin talking about your faith with a seeker, it is often most effective to just tell a slice of your own story. Your story could be about how Jesus has taken you from a meaningless existence to a life filled with purpose. Or about how Jesus has brought a depth of joy to your life that you never experienced before. Or about how your faith has given you strength to seek restoration in relationships. Your story could be about anything God has done in your life since you became a follower of Jesus.

As you build friendships with seekers, listen closely and you will discover their points of need. You already know Jesus is the One who can fill the void in their life. Through your testimony, address one or two ways Jesus has met these deep needs in *your* life, and let your seeking friend know Jesus can do the same for them. This kind of testimony is nonthreatening but very salty. It creates in them a thirst to meet this Jesus who can satisfy their deepest needs.

Read Snapshot "Do vs. Done" before Question 5

Question Five Here is a more detailed walk through of the "Do vs. Done" illustration. You may want to read this to group members:

In the course of a conversation, you might say, "Mary, if you'd ever be interested in discovering the difference between religion and Christianity, I'd be happy to talk to you about it." If she responds with openness, you continue, "Well, Mary, religion is spelled D-O. Religion is all about trying to *do* things to gain God's approval, to earn eternal life, even to make up for past sins. Religion is about doing things in the hope that if you do enough, you can earn God's favor. You know, Mary, that's a dead-end road. Because you don't ever know if you've done enough. You're never told what the quota is. How much is enough? And if you just try to do more and more, you discover it's never enough."

You might then say to her, "Mary, think with me. Would a loving God play those kinds of games with people? Would He make us earn our way to heaven by doing good things, but not tell us whether or not we have done enough? I don't believe He would."

At this point, she is probably more than ready to hear what you have to say about Christianity. Religion has been uncovered as a dead-end street. If she seems responsive, continue on and tell her about Christianity.

"Christianity is spelled D-O-N-E! Christianity says 'No one can measure up to God's standard of holiness. No amount of effort or sacrifice can merit God's favor or eternal life.' You see, Mary, people cannot save themselves by doing good deeds. When Jesus died on the cross, He said, 'It is finished. I've done it.' Jesus has done something you could never do for yourself. He's paid the price for your sin. Through His death and resurrection, God has made a way for us to be acceptable in His sight. In Jesus we realize it is D-O-N-E!"

If this seems to make sense to her, you can walk her through the Gospel: "You know, Mary, if you receive the gift of forgiveness that comes from what Christ has done for you on the cross, you can become a Christian. You can live with the assurance that you will go to heaven when you die. You can be born again."

Read Snapshot "The Bridge" before Question 6

Question Six This illustration is so simple a child can learn it. It is helpful because it allows people to picture the situation. You don't have to be an artist to use this illustration. As a matter of fact, the strength of this illustration is its simplicity.

Draw a valley with you on one side and God on the other. Explain how sin stands between you and God. Then point out that human effort can't get you across. Any human effort to leap across the valley will cause us to fall to our death. You might even want to write the word "death" across the bottom of the valley. No matter how far we think we can get on our own strength, the end result will be the same. We can't make it on our own. You may want to read Romans 6:23 at this time: "The wages of sin is death."

Now explain that Jesus is the only bridge that can span the distance between us and God. Draw the vertical line of the cross up and down right through the middle of the word "death" as a statement of God's power over it. Then, draw the horizontal line of the cross from one side of the valley to the other. This shows that the cross of Jesus and His sacrificial death make it possible for us to be restored to relationship with our heavenly Father. Explain that Jesus has done the work, and that all we need to do is receive His finished work and cross the bridge.

You may want to ask how close the person is to stepping onto the bridge. You can point to the very edge of the cliff and say, "Are you this close?" You may want to point back somewhat from the edge and ask if they are standing back there. Try to discover how close they sense they are to accepting what Jesus has done for them.

Read Snapshot "The Roman Road" before Question 7

Question Seven Here is an example of how this Gospel presentation can be used:

Have the three critical texts from Romans underlined in your Bible. Say, "John, would you like to know how you can become a Christian? I'm not saying you have to become one right now, but would you like to know how in case you decide to?" You are there to present the message; it's God's job to do the work of conversion.

If John is interested, walk with him down The Roman Road.

You might say to him, "John, let's read Romans 3:23." Turn your Bible around and let him read it: "For all have sinned and fall short of the glory of God," at which time simply say, "John, did you notice the word 'all'? All have sinned. I want to tell you something. I'm in that 'all'. Are you? Have you sinned before a holy God?" You might want to briefly explain that sinning is any time we come short of God's perfect standard. It can even be helpful to give him a few examples.

Then say, "Now, John, let's turn to Romans 6:23." Turn to this passage in your Bible and say, "Would you read this one too?" John reads, "For the wages of sin is death, but the gift of God is eternal life in Christ Jesus our Lord." Ask him, "John, what are wages? "Well," John says, "They're what you get for working, rewards for laboring." Then ask him, "John, what does this text say the wages of doing sin are?" If he responds according to this passage, he will say, "death." Then you respond, "Well, John, what that means is two kinds of death. There is physical death—you're not going to be here a hundred years from now and neither am I. Because of sin, we die physically. But the Bible also talks about a spiritual death, and that means a separation from God in hell for eternity."

Then say, "John, I hope you noticed there is also good news in this verse. It says, 'The gift of God is eternal life in Christ Jesus our Lord.' What's a gift, John?"

"Well," he might say, "a gift is something somebody gives you."

"Do you have to work for it, John?"

"No, no, if you work for it, then a gift would be wages."

Then ask him, "John, what free gift is God offering you?"

"Well, the free gift of God is eternal life."

"That's right, and who offers you this free gift?"

He might say something like, "Well, this seems to say it's through Jesus Christ."

At this, tell him, "John, God offers you the free gift of salvation, eternal life, and forgiveness of sin. It comes only through the death and the resurrection of Jesus Christ. John, listen to me. You matter to God more than you'll ever know. You have sinned against Him and you have earned the wages of sin— death. But because you matter to God, because Jesus took your wages and absorbed your punishment on the cross, a free gift is being offered to you. You can't work for it, you can't earn it, you can't buy it, you can't brag about it, you can only receive it. And when you receive it, you're forgiven and you're cleansed. You get eternal life. Sounds too good to be true, doesn't it, John? But it is true."

Finally, focus on one last verse that explains how he can receive this gift if that is what he desires. Say, "John, let's read just one more verse." Turn to Romans 10:13 and have John read, "Everyone who calls on the name of the Lord will be saved." Then ask the simple question, "Does *everyone* even mean someone like you, John? Do you fit into that category? All you have to do to be saved is to call upon the name of the Lord."

If he seems open and receptive, say, "All you have to do is pray, John. Just say, 'Lord Jesus, I'm a sinner. I own up to it. I understand the wages of sin is death, physical death and spiritual death, and that's what I deserve. But I thank You for offering the free gift of forgiveness, cleansing, and eternal life through the price Jesus paid for my sin on the cross. And now Lord, I accept that gift. I need it; I request it; I receive it by faith."

Sometimes you might want to say, "John, why don't we just pray right now? Are you ready? Call upon the name of the Lord right now and just say, 'I'm a sinner who is ready to receive the free gift of salvation through Jesus Christ, and I ask right now for the free gift of salvation through Jesus Christ.'"

Question Eight If you have time left and group members feel comfortable doing it, you may want to have them pair up and practice whichever method they feel most comfortable with on each other. Try to make it light and fun; don't get too intense. This could stretch the comfort zone of some in your group. But the more you practice these methods of communicating the faith, the more effective and comfortable you will become.

PUTTING YOURSELF IN THE PICTURE

Challenge group members to take time in the coming week to use part or all of this application section as an opportunity for continued growth.

DISCOVERING YOUR STYLE: PART 1

Acts 17:16–34;, Acts 2:14, 36; John 9

INTRODUCTION

The key to this entire study guide is helping people discover the evangelism style that fits them. For too long, the church has called people to go out and be evangelists but has failed to help them discover how they should do it. God has wired each of us differently. Each of us has a style somewhat different from the other. However, there are some general styles that will help your small group members begin to identify how they can most effectively explain their faith.

In this session we look at the three specific styles of evangelism most often identified as the standard way for Christians to do evangelism. People with a confrontational style put the message right on the table. Those with an intellectual style are very comfortable explaining the truth of the Bible and the meaning of the Christian faith. And people who have a testimonial style do evangelism by telling their personal stories of faith, helping others see the presence and power of God in their lives. As we look at these three styles, we will study a biblical example of each, as well as take steps for group members to begin identifying their particular style.

THE BIG PICTURE

Take time to read this introduction with the group. There are suggestions for how this can be done in the beginning of this leader's section.

A WIDE ANGLE VIEW

Question One Only a tiny fraction of the unbelievers in this world will be reached by the stereotypical evangelist.

The hellfire and brimstone preacher will reach some, and God has blessed the church with those who can effectively lead evangelistic crusades. However, the unbelieving world is made up of such a variety of people that no one approach can reach everyone—young and old, rich and poor, educated and uneducated, urban and rural, different races, personalities, values, political systems, religious backgrounds. Isn't it obvious that no single style of evangelism, and certainly no single evangelist, would ever be able to relate to such a diverse population? This is why every single believer is so important. Through our individual style and approach, we can all reach different people.

A BIBLICAL PORTRAIT

Read Acts 17:16–34

Question Two Paul used an intellectual style of evangelism. This style was effective because it fit the people he was trying to reach.

SHARPENING THE FOCUS

Read Snapshot "Intellectual Style" before Question 3

Questions Three & Four Paul was highly educated, extremely intelligent, and capable of putting together cogent arguments. He knew some people needed their questions answered before they could come to Christ. Paul loved thinking, studying, contemplating, and reasoning. This is the way God wired him.

The church has been blessed with many brilliant people who can intellectually explain the faith in a way that reaches seekers. Josh McDowell, known worldwide for having that same kind of ministry, wrote the book *Evidence That Demands a Verdict*. Many believers today, much like the apostle Paul or people like Josh McDowell, can be very effective evangelists for those who need answers and evidence. If this is your style, develop it. Read good books on this topic. Practice talking about Jesus in a way that answers hard questions about faith. Talk with others who have this same approach and learn from them. Sharpen your abilities and pray for opportunities to communicate your faith.

Question Five Once your group members have identified specific people they feel could be reached by someone with an intellectual style of evangelism, take time to pray for these seekers. Also pray for group members who are reaching out to those seekers.

If there are any members of your group who believe they have this style of evangelism, allow them to take a few minutes to communicate how they would convey the Gospel to a seeker who needed this style of evangelism.

If you have identified a seeker who needs an intellectual presentation of the Gospel and a person in your group who has this approach, find a natural and comfortable way to introduce these two people and begin praying for God to provide a place for the message of Jesus to be communicated in a way that person can understand.

Read Snapshot "Confrontational Style" before Question 6

Questions Six & Seven Some of us are a lot like Peter. We're action people. Remember, it was Peter who almost always responded first when Jesus asked a question. Peter was the only one who got out of the boat and was willing to try walking on the water. In the garden, when Jesus was arrested, Peter took his sword and cut off the ear of the servant of the high priest. Peter loved action. He liked to stir up controversy. It really didn't bother Peter to stand up on Pentecost Day and say, "You better all listen to me." Who better than Peter to do that kind of thing? It fit him perfectly. This is the way God wired this bold fisherman.

The truth is, some lost people in this world are only going to come to Christ if they are confronted boldly with the truth. And guess what? God created some of us a lot like Peter.

Think of Chuck Colson. He's amazing. He just says "I think it's high time some of you face the music, because if you don't have Jesus Christ as your Savior, you're on the road to hell. Unless you repent of your sins, admit it, get down on your knees and trust Christ, you're in deep weeds forever." I don't think afterward Chuck says, "Was I too hard on them?" I think Chuck says, "Did I hit them hard enough?" The truth is, lots of people have come to Christ through Chuck Colson. Billy Graham is a lot like this also. He just lays the message of salvation on the line and lets people respond.

Some people might just need you to look them right in the eye and say, "So what about it? Are you ready to meet Jesus?" If this is you, start looking for opportunities, create a little action, mix it up, do it! There are people out there that only people like you can reach.

Question Eight Once your group members have identified specific people they feel could be reached by someone with a confrontational style of evangelism, take time to pray for these seekers. Also pray for group members who are reaching out to those seekers.

If there are any members of your group who believe they have this style of evangelism, allow them to take a few minutes to communicate how they would convey the Gospel to a seeker who needed this style of evangelism.

If you have identified a seeker who needs a confrontational presentation of the Gospel and a person in your group who has this approach, find a natural and comfortable way to introduce these two people and begin praying for God to provide a place for the message of Jesus to be communicated in a way that person can understand.

Read Snapshot "Testimonial Style" before Question 9

Question Nine Many followers of Christ, like the blind man, have witnessed dramatic changes in their lives. Seekers need to hear these stories of change and transformation. There are lots of people who won't respond to confrontation or to an intellectual argument, but who would just love to hear one solid, sane person tell a true story of how Jesus Christ changed a human life. There are tons of people waiting for someone like you, with your personality, age, professional background, and temperament to just tell your story of faith. It might be only a three- or four-minute story, but it holds the key to what has changed your life.

Question Eleven Once your group members have identified specific people they feel could be reached by someone with an testimonial style of evangelism, take time to pray for these seekers. Also pray for group members who are reaching out to those seekers.

If there are any members of your group who believe they have this style of evangelism, allow them to take a few minutes to communicate how they would convey the Gospel to a seeker who needed this style of evangelism.

If you have identified a seeker who needs a testimonial presentation of the Gospel and a person in your group who has this approach, find a natural and comfortable way to introduce these two people and begin praying for God to provide a place for the message of Jesus to be communicated in a way that person can understand.

Note: There are many varied styles of spreading the message of Christ. But the heart of this session is that all the various styles are essential if we're going to reach all of the lost people of this world. No one style is going to do it. God made you just the way He did in part so that there would be someone just like you with a style just like yours to reach some lost person who will not respond to any style of witness other than yours. If you would just penetrate your heart with these truths, you would look at evangelism a whole new way. Stop thinking that because you're not a Billy Graham, you cannot be effective in evangelism. Stop thinking you have to become someone you were not created to be. You simply need to be who God made you to be, identify your particular style*, and get on with the task of spreading the message of Christ in the power of the Holy Spirit.

PUTTING YOURSELF IN THE PICTURE

Challenge group members to take time in the coming week to use part or all of this application section as an opportunity for continued growth.

*The *Becoming a Contagious Christian* training course has further information and an individualized questionnaire to help each person discover and develop their own evangelism style. For further information on the course, see the information pages in the back of this book.

DISCOVERING YOUR STYLE: PART 2

Luke 5:27–32; John 4; Acts 9

INTRODUCTION

Just as in last week's session, we will look at three styles of evangelism. The key is to help group members understand there is no set pattern or formula into which they have to fit. God has wired them just the way they are so they can reach a specific kind of person. Pray for each group member to discover a style that fits them and to get excited about telling others about Jesus.

THE BIG PICTURE

Take time to read this introduction with the group. There are suggestions for how this can be done in the beginning of this leader's section.

A WIDE ANGLE VIEW

Question One Allow for honest expression of fears. As we face these fears and articulate them, we can begin to offer them to God. It might be helpful at this time to pause and pray for God to give each member of the group courage and freedom from fear when it comes to being an evangelist.

A BIBLICAL PORTRAIT

Read Luke 5:27–32

SHARPENING THE FOCUS

Read Snapshot "Interpersonal Style" before Question 3

Questions Three & Four Many followers of Christ feel left out of the whole task of evangelism because they don't feel they can confront or give intellectual arguments or give testimonials. Maybe their style is as simple as getting the right people together. These people have a passion for creating opportunities for relationships and networking. We need to encourage this approach to evangelism and realize it is just as powerful and Spirit-led as the boldest confrontational presentation of the Gospel or the most articulate argument or most fluent testimony.

Read Snapshot "Invitational Style" before Question 5

Questions Five & Six Maybe God intends for you to do exactly what the woman at the well did. She just passed out an invitation. If your style is invitational, you can say, "Come and hear. I'm not very good at explaining it. I can't be intellectual about it. I'm not the confrontational type. I'm not even that relational, but come and see, come and hear."

If this is your style, start getting creative. Discover anything and everything you can invite seekers to attend. It might be a small group, a seeker-sensitive worship service, a Christian concert, a money management class, a dramatic presentation. Any time you go to an event where Christ will be honored, think about inviting a friend who is a seeker to come along.

Stop saying, "Because I can't be confrontational, I can't count in the work of evangelism." You can be enormously effective. The woman at the well changed half her town by just saying, "Come and see, come and hear." A woman approached me one evening after a service and said, "You know, I'm trying my best to fill a row. I can't do evangelism very well, but I can fill a row and have them hear you talk about Christ. So that's my goal, to fill a row." I'm telling you, there is a tremendous ministry in evangelism through invitations.

Read Snapshot "Service Style" before Question 7

Questions Seven & Eight Some followers of Christ have tender spirits and helpful hearts. Their gifts are those of service, mercy, hospitality, counseling, and giving. People with these gifts can be very effective evangelists as they share Christ by serving people.

One time I was driving someplace in the middle of a snowstorm, and the car in front of me stalled. It was right in the middle of an intersection, so I got out and helped push his car off to the side of the road. I had a phone in my car, so I said, "Would you like to use my phone to call for help?" And he said, "I really would." After he called for help, he put the phone down and said, "What could I possibly do to repay you?" I said, "Well, you know what you could do? It was a joy to help you, and I'm not bribing you or anything, but if you really want to do something, visit Willow Creek Community Church one time." He said, "That's funny. I don't go to church, but I've heard about that church, and I was thinking about going there. I guess I just needed a push." True story! Sometimes an act of service can be a great way to communicate the love of Jesus.

One of our people on the mercy team had an opportunity to lead someone with a terminal illness to Christ. That person's visiting and encouragement connected service with evangelism and led someone to Christ. That simple act was worth so much in the scope of eternity!

Don't put yourselves down and say, "You know, all I can do is just serve people." If you can serve people, you have an incredibly effective lead-in to sharing Christ.

Question Nine Review your leader's notes on each of these six styles. You might also want to use the book and/or training course entitled *Becoming a Contagious Christian* as a resource.

CLOSING

You might want to close your group with this prayer:

Father, we have come to realize that there's not a person in this group who doesn't have a part to play in the greatest endeavor on this planet—reaching lost people with the Good News of Christ. I pray that people would stop putting themselves down, stop saying they can't participate, they don't have the talent, skills, or abilities. I pray we would identify who You made us to be and become energized by the power of the Holy Spirit. I pray we would use our own individual style to reach who You've called us to reach. I pray with fervency for the work of evangelism in our workplaces, neighborhoods, and our families. May we all do our part in reaching people for the kingdom in Jesus' name. Amen.

ADDITIONAL WILLOW CREEK RESOURCES

Small Group Resources

Leading Life-Changing Small Groups, by Bill Donahue

The Walking with God Series, by Don Cousins and Judson Poling

Evangelism Resources

Becoming a Contagious Christian (book), by Bill Hybels and Mark Mittelberg

Becoming a Contagious Christian (training course), by Mark Mittelberg, Lee Strobel, and Bill Hybels

God's Outrageous Claims by Lee Strobel

Inside the Mind of Unchurched Harry and Mary, by Lee Strobel

Inside the Soul of a New Generation, by Tim Celek and Dieter Zander, with Patrick Kampert

The Journey: A Bible for Seeking God and Understanding Life

What Jesus Would Say, by Lee Strobel

Spiritual Gifts and Ministry

Network (training course), by Bruce Bugbee, Don Cousins, and Bill Hybels

What You Do Best, by Bruce Bugbee

Marriage & Parenting

Fit to Be Tied, by Bill and Lynne Hybels

Authenticity

Honest to God?, by Bill Hybels

Descending into Greatness, by Bill Hybels

Ministry Resources

Rediscovering Church, by Bill Hybels

The Source, compiled by Scott Dyer, introduction by Nancy Beach

Sunday Morning Live, edited by Steve Pederson

Christianity 101, by Gilbert Bilezikian

All of these resources are published in association with Zondervan Publishing House

More evangelism resources from Willow Creek

Becoming a Contagious Christian
Bill Hybels and Mark Mittelberg

This landmark book articulates the central principles of relational evangelism that have helped Willow Creek Community Church become a church known around the world for its outstanding outreach to unchurched people. Based on the words of Jesus and flowing from the firsthand experiences of the authors, *Becoming a Contagious Christian* presents a groundbreaking, personalized approach to evangelism that will transform your personal witness to those in your life who don't yet know Christ.

Softcover: 0-310-21008-9
Also available on audio cassette: 0-310-48508-8

Becoming a Contagious Christian Training Course
Communicating Your Faith in a Style that Fits You
Mark Mittelberg, Lee Strobel, and Bill Hybels

Expanding on the book, this hands-on training course helps ordinary Christians develop confidence and skills that enable them to effectively share the Gospel with people they know. Designed especially for those who think evangelism is not for them, this curriculum is a powerful tool for equipping those in your small group, Sunday school, or entire church to naturally communicate their faith in a way that's contagious! Its clear and detailed Leader's Guide, combined with the overheads and the video of brief, real-life drama vignettes, makes this course easy for anyone in your church to lead.

Kit includes: • 60-minute Video   • Participant's Guide
                 • Leader's Guide   • Overhead Masters

Curriculum Kit: 0-310-50109-1
Participant's Guide also available separately: 0-310-50101-6

Look for Becoming a Contagious Christian *book, audio, and training course at your local Christian bookstore.*

ZondervanPublishingHouse
Grand Rapids, Michigan

A Division of HarperCollins*Publishers*

Finally! A Bible specifically designed for your unchurched friends.

The Journey
A Bible for Seeking God & Understanding Life

The Journey is the perfect resource to give to friends looking for answers to life's big questions. Including introductory articles, book introductions, a reading plan, and more, it is uniquely designed to help spiritual seekers and younger believers discover the practical aspects of Christianity and better understand God. More than 450 icon-tagged information windows track six themes that are key to the questions so many people are asking: "Discovering God," "Addressing Questions," "Strengthening Relationships," "Reasons to Believe," "Knowing Yourself," and "Managing Resources." All these helps are combined with the popular and trusted New International Version (NIV) text of the Bible to create a readable, relevant presentation of God's truth to those who are seeking to know more about Him. Share your faith and start your friends on *The Journey*.

Hardcover: 0-310-91949-5
Softcover: 0-310-91950-9

Intriguing reading for believer and seeker alike!

What Jesus Would Say
To: Rush Limbaugh, Madonna, Bill Clinton, Michael Jordan, Bart Simpson, Donald Trump, Murphy Brown, Madalyn Murray O'Hair, Mother Teresa, David Letterman, and YOU!

Lee Strobel

Did you ever wonder what Jesus might say to today's movers and shakers, celebrities, and opinion-makers? Lee Strobel did, and he takes an educated guess in this intriguing and thought-provoking book. In it, he helps us see well-known personalities as Jesus might see them, while tackling topics like success, sexuality, skepticism, forgiveness, prayer, and leadership with firm, biblically-based concepts. And through it all, he reintroduces us to the God of hope, the God of the second chance. *What Jesus Would Say* has been reviewed and discussed in 200 newspapers around the world. Needless to say, it is stimulating reading for believer and seeker alike.

Softcover: 0-310-48511-8
Also available on audio cassette: 0-310-48518-5

Look for The Journey *and* What Jesus Would Say
at your local Christian bookstore.

ZondervanPublishingHouse
Grand Rapids, Michigan

A Division of HarperCollins*Publishers*

WILLOW CREEK RESOURCES

To reach them effectively,
you have to know them intimately

Inside the Mind of Unchurched Harry & Mary
How to Reach Friends and Family Who Avoid God and the Church
Lee Strobel

Who are Unchurched Harry and Mary? The neighbor who seems perfectly happy without God; the coworker who scoffs at Christianity; the supervisor who uses Jesus' name only as profanity; or the family member who can't understand why religion is so important. Lee Strobel knows this person well—he once was one himself. In this timely, Gold Medallion Award-winning book, Strobel uses personal experiences, humor, compelling stories, biblical illustrations, and the latest research to help Christians understand unbelievers and what motivates them. Not a book of theory, *Inside the Mind...* is an action plan to help Christians relate the message of Christ to the people they work around, live with, and value as friends.

Softcover: 0-310-37561-4
Also available on audio cassette: 0-310-61498-8

Inside the Soul of a New Generation
Insights and Strategies for Reaching Busters
Tim Celek and Dieter Zander, with Patrick Kampert

Generation X. Busters. This is the group of 46 million Americans born between 1965 and 1980. Through years of experience in Buster ministry, Celek and Zander have learned invaluable lessons about how to win this generation of young people. *Inside the Soul of a New Generation* offers a fascinating look at the unique forces that have shaped this generation and shows how pastors, parents, and baby boomers can minister to their spiritual needs, bring them into the church, and develop them into mature leaders who will be able to reach yet another new generation.

Softcover: 0-310-20594-8

Look for Inside the Mind of Unchurched Harry & Mary *and*
Inside the Soul of a New Generation *at your local Christian bookstore*

ZondervanPublishingHouse
Grand Rapids, Michigan

A Division of HarperCollinsPublishers

WILLOW
CREEK
RESOURCES

WILLOW CREEK
RESOURCES

This resource was created to serve you.

It is just one of many ministry tools that are part of the Willow Creek Resources® line, published by the Willow Creek Association together with Zondervan Publishing House. The Willow Creek Association was created in 1992 to serve a rapidly growing number of churches from all across the denominational spectrum that are committed to helping unchurched people become fully devoted followers of Christ. There are now more than 2,500 WCA member churches worldwide.

The Willow Creek Association links like-minded leaders with each other and with strategic vision, information, and resources in order to build prevailing churches. Here are some of the ways it does that:

- Church Leadership Conferences—3 1/2 -day events, held at Willow Creek Community Church in South Barrington, IL, that are being used by God to help church leaders find new and innovative ways to build prevailing churches that reach unchurched people.

- The Leadership Summit—a once-a-year event designed to increase the leadership effectiveness of pastors, ministry staff, volunteer church leaders, and Christians in business.

- Willow Creek Resources®—to provide churches with a trusted channel of ministry resources in areas of leadership, evangelism, spiritual gifts, small groups, drama, contemporary music, and more. For more information, call Willow Creek Resources® at 800/876-7335. Outside the US call 610/532-1249.

- *WCA News*—a bimonthly newsletter to inform you of the latest trends, resources, and information on WCA events from around the world.

- *The Exchange*—our classified ads publication to assist churches in recruiting key staff for ministry positions.

- The Church Associates Directory—to keep you in touch with other WCA member churches around the world.

- *WillowNet*—an Internet service that provides access to hundreds of Willow Creek messages, drama scripts, songs, videos and multimedia suggestions. The system allows users to sort through these elements and download them for a fee.

- *Defining Moments*—a monthly audio journal for church leaders, in which Lee Strobel asks Bill Hybels and other Christian leaders probing questions to help you discover biblical principles and transferable strategies to help maximize your church's potential.

For conference and membership information please write or call:

Willow Creek Association
P.O. Box 3188
Barrington, IL 60011-3188
ph: (847) 765-0070
fax: (847) 765-5046
www.willowcreek.org

0597